Workshops for
JAIL LIBRARY SERVICE
A Planning Manual

LINDA SCHEXNAYDRE
KAYLYN ROBBINS

PREPARED FOR THE ASSOCIATION OF SPECIALIZED
AND COOPERATIVE LIBRARY AGENCIES
A DIVISION OF THE AMERICAN LIBRARY ASSOCIATION

WITHDRAWN

AMERICAN LIBRARY ASSOCIATION
Chicago 1981

Copyright is claimed until 1986. Thereafter all portions of this work covered by this copyright will be in the public domain.

This work was developed under a grant from the Department of Education. However, the content does not necessarily reflect the position or policy of that agency and no official endorsement of these materials should be inferred.

Library of Congress Cataloging in Publication Data

Schexnaydre, Linda.
  Workshops for jail library service.

  Bibliography: p.
  1. Prison libraries—Congresses.   2. Library institutes and workshops.
I. Robbins, Kaylyn.   II. Title.
Z675.P8S34   020'.7'15   81-1041
ISBN 0-8389-3529-2   AACR2

Copyright © 1981 by the American Library Association

All rights reserved. No part of this publication may be reproduced in any form without permission in writing from the publisher, except by a reviewer who may quote brief passages in a review.

Printed in the United States of America

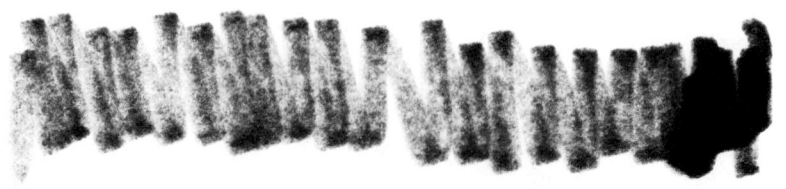

To Connie House
 *Because of the vision of jail library service
  that she shared during three exciting years.*

Contents

Forms	vii
Preface	ix
How to Use This Manual	xi

Section 1. Planning the Workshop 1

The Planners	1
Workshop Coordinator	1
Sponsors	2
Planning Committee	3
Workshop Timeline	6
The Participants	9
Selecting Participant Groups	9
Encouraging Participation by Sheriff-Librarian Teams	10
Workshop Content	11
Assessing What Practitioners Need to Learn	11
Selecting a Workshop	16
Workshop Objectives	17
Designing the Workshop	18
Resource People and Trainers	18
Workshop Evaluation	20
Logistics	21
Workshop Length	21
Choosing Workshop Dates	21
Deciding on Locations	23
Selecting Facilities	23
Site Coordinator	23
Publicity	24
Budgeting	24

Section 2. Conducting the Workshop   29

Using the Workshop Designs   29
    Materials   30
    Training Techniques   30

Books behind Bars   32
    Introduction   32
    Workshop Design   36
    Materials   41

Establishing Jail Library Service   46
    Introduction   46
    Workshop Design   59
    Materials   69

Jail Library Service Is More than Books   75
    Introduction   75
    Workshop Ideas   78

Conference on Improving Jail Library Service   80
    Introduction   80
    Conference Design   83

Appendixes
    A. Human Resources for Improving Jail Library Service   87
    B. The Jail Library Game   93
    C. Jail and Prison Films and Other Nonprint Materials   105

Further Readings   115

Forms

A.	Sponsors Worksheet	4
B.	Jail Library Service: A Questionnaire	13
C.	Jail Library Service: A Questionnaire	14
D.	Jail Library Service: Workshop Report Form	22
E.	Publicity Worksheet	25
F.	Budget Worksheet	27

Books behind Bars

G.	Sample Publicity Flyer	34
H.	Sample Agenda	35
I.	Jail Library Service: Who to Contact	42
J.	Jail Library Service: What to Do in Your Local Community	43
K.	Evaluation Form	44
L.	Jail Library Service: Request for Further Information	45

Establishing Jail Library Service

M.	Sample Publicity Flyer	49
N.	Preregistration Form	50
O.	Sample Workshop Announcement	52
P.	Sample Memo	53
Q.	Gathering Information about Your Jail	54
R.	Gathering Information about Your Library	56
S.	Sample Agenda	58
T.	Daily Reaction Form	66
U.	Plan for Jail Library Service Feedback Sheet	68
V.	Report on Plan for Jail Library Service	71
W.	Evaluation Form	72
X.	Jail Library Service: Request for Further Information and Training	74

Jail Library Service Is More than Books
    Y. Sample Agenda   77

Conference on Improving Jail Library Service
    Z. Sample Agenda   82

Preface

During 1979–80 the Association of Specialized and Cooperative Library Agencies (a division of the American Library Association) received an HEA II-B grant for a project entitled "Improving Jail Library Service," co-sponsored by the American Correctional Association, the National Jail Association, the National Sheriffs Association, the Fortune Society, and the Texas Criminal Justice Center at Sam Houston State University. This project was designed for jail staff, librarians, community agency personnel, local officials, and anyone else who believes that jail library service can provide the framework for overall education and rehabilitation of inmates and improved jail conditions and services. One of the significant aspects of this project is that correctional personnel, ex-offenders, and librarians were involved from the beginning.

The major products from this year of funding are:

* *Jail Library Service: A Guide for Librarians and Jail Administrators.* ALA, 1981. Project director, Sandra M. Cooper.

A step-by-step guide for jail and library staff on how to initiate or improve local jail library service. It also provides the content for workshops on jail library service.

* *Workshops for Jail Library Service: A Planning Manual.* ALA, 1981. Project director, Connie House.

A guide to planning and conducting workshops, conference programs, preconferences, institutes, and staff development sessions on jail library service for jail staff, library staff, other community agency personnel, and interested volunteers. *Jail Library Service* provides the content for the workshops in this manual.

---

*Available from ALA, 50 E. Huron, Chicago, IL 60611

National Institute on Library Service to Jail Populations. Huntsville, Texas, March 9–12, 1980. Project director, Connie House.

The National Institute trained 100 librarians, jail personnel, and state agency consultants in current trends and issues in jail library service and examined a number of problem areas. Videotapes of the institute sessions are available. For more information contact ASCLA, ALA, 50 E. Huron St., Chicago, IL 60611.

How to Use This Manual

WORKSHOPS FOR JAIL LIBRARY SERVICE is the companion volume to *Jail Library Service: A Guide for Librarians and Jail Administrators*. The content of *Jail Library Service* will be used by planners and workshop leaders to design the workshops discussed in this manual. We recommend that you read *Jail Library Service* before beginning to work with this manual.

Jail library service workshops can be planned by a variety of groups—jail personnel, librarians, former inmates, other community groups or state agency personnel. Participants attending the workshops will represent these same diverse groups. Because jail library service is relatively new and workshop participants come from a variety of fields, this manual has been written to provide you with options for planning and designing the content of your workshop.

Since jail library service involves jail staff and librarians, the most effective training takes place when both groups plan and attend the same workshop. This manual contains suggestions for involving both groups in workshop planning, publicity, evaluation, and as workshop participants and speakers. If it is not possible for you to include both groups in your workshop, this manual suggests how the training can be adapted for either jail personnel or librarians. Speakers and resource people should always represent both the corrections and library fields, however.

This manual contains step-by-step information on how to plan your workshop and ideas for how to conduct different types of workshops. See pages 16 and 17 for a description of workshops included in this manual. If you are on the workshop planning committee, you may be most interested in Section 1, Planning the Workshop. If you are deciding on the content and organization of the workshop, you may be more interested in Section 2, Conducting the Workshop, which includes the four different workshop outlines. Workshop planning and workshop design are equally critical to the success of your workshop; however, you may not be equally involved in both activities. Page references have been provided throughout the text to get you back and forth between the two sections as needed.

We hope this manual will be of special use to the novice or beginning trainer-practitioners in the jail and library fields who become involved in sharing their expertise with others as planners or workshop leaders. Novice workshop leaders may want to work through this manual step-by-step and refer to additional readings that have been listed in the bibliography. The information on working with jail and library personnel will make it easier for more experienced trainers to plan workshops that will attract both groups.

Two sections in this manual are particularly important. Using the Workshop Designs describes our basic approach to designing workshops. Whether you want to use a workshop design as is or modify it, you will want to read this section to get an overall understanding of what the workshops contain. For more information about the organizations and institutions referred to in this manual, including abbreviations, consult Appendix A, Human Resources for Jail Library Service. This directory suggests how you can contact jail personnel, librarians, and ex-offenders in your state to find out about the current status of jail library service. Much of this information has been pulled together as a result of the National Institute on Library Service to Jail Populations and through the efforts of Connie House, project director.

Many of the ideas for workshop content and the suggestions for involving library and jail staff in jail library service workshops have come from our experiences in working with the National Institute on Library Service to Jail Populations. For those who were unable to attend the National Institute, we hope to share some of the institute materials and training techniques to encourage you to plan and conduct your own jail library service workshops. The "Conference on Improving Jail Library Service" in Section 2 most closely resembles the institute. For those who attended the National Institute, we hope that this manual will make it easier for you to share what you know about jail library service.

We are also interested in hearing from you about the workshops that you provide. Please complete the Jail Library Service: Workshop Report Form (p. 22) after your workshop, and return it to ASCLA so that others can benefit from your ideas and experiences.

ASSOCIATION OF SPECIALIZED AND COOPERATIVE
LIBRARY AGENCIES
AMERICAN LIBRARY ASSOCIATION
50 East Huron
Chicago, Illinois 60611

Section 1

Planning the Workshop

The Planners

There are a variety of people involved in planning a workshop. This section identifies these individuals and delineates the tasks they need to accomplish. How these tasks are divided among the planners—the workshop coordinator, the sponsors, and the planning committee—will vary. Do not be overwhelmed by the complexity of the planning process in this section. It has been designed to be adequate for a two- or three-day workshop. If you are planning a short or local program, many of these steps will be unnecessary; the time frame can be shortened, and the number of planners reduced.

Workshop Coordinator

One person must have overall responsibility for coordinating and supervising all those involved in preparing for and conducting the workshop. This person is called the workshop coordinator. Major responsibilities of the workshop coordinator are:

1. Working closely with the sponsors and planning committee to plan the workshop, deciding on workshop content, publicizing adequately to both librarians and jail personnel, and budgeting for an effective program.
2. Designing workshop activities or locating subject specialists and trainers to take responsibility for these matters.
3. Locating and working with speakers, small group leaders, and other resource people before and during the workshop.
4. Delegating local arrangements to a site coordinator who will take care of all details pertaining to the workshop facilities. The site coordinator should also attend the workshop to be sure that all arrangements are being properly taken care of.
5. Coordinating all details and activities during the workshop and relying on subject specialists, speakers, trainers, small group leaders to conduct the workshop.

6. Evaluating the workshop, possibly with an outside evaluator.
7. Delegating all other workshop tasks, monitoring their completion according to schedule, and troubleshooting when necessary.

A more detailed list of workshop tasks—to be accomplished before, during, and after the workshop—is found in the timeline on pages 6–9. Most of these tasks can be delegated to others, who report at regular intervals to the workshop coordinator.

Since many workshop details are clerical in nature, the coordinator needs secretarial assistance (possibly from the home institution or from a sponsor) for mailouts, correspondence, phone calls, typing, and assistance in organizing and keeping track of details. For a more complex workshop, the coordinator needs release time or a job assignment relating to the workshop so that work time can be available for coordinating workshop plans. It will also be useful if the workshop coordinator has some previous workshop experience.

Workshop coordinators with little or no experience in planning and conducting workshops should consult the bibliography on page 115 of this manual, especially:

> Larry Davis, *Planning, Conducting, Evaluating Workshops* (Learning Concepts, 1974).
> Ruth Warncke, *Planning Library Workshops and Institutes* (ALA, 1976).

Sponsors

Sponsors for jail library service workshops are most frequently professional associations, state agencies, library systems, and criminal justice institutes. Workshops can also be sponsored by local public libraries and jails. Sometimes the sponsor first becomes aware of the training need and has the capability to get the planning started. In this case, the sponsor will be involved in forming the planning committee and may designate one of its staff as the workshop coordinator. At other times, interest in training for jail library service can come from practitioners who then need to find a sponsor. If you are interested in a workshop on jail library service and do not have a sponsor, look for:

> Sponsors in both corrections and library fields
> Groups that have high visibility and credibility with public librarians and jail personnel
> Groups that represent workshop participants
> Groups that may be able to provide funds for training, publicity, subject specialists, and facilities for the workshop.

Possible sponsors in your area:

1. State library agencies usually provide some type of continuing education for libraries in the state, have money to support work-

shops, have consultants with experience as library trainers, and have mechanisms set up to handle workshop publicity, mailing lists, and newsletters.
2. State correctional agencies have consultants and funds for training and have mechanisms set up to handle workshop publicity, mailing lists, and newsletters. Some also have training academies.
3. Library systems, where they exist, usually have consultants and some money for workshops for libraries within their geographic area, have consultants with some experience as library trainers, and have mechanisms set up to publicize workshops within their regional area.
4. State or regional library associations, state correctional associations, and state sheriffs associations usually have annual conferences at which programs can be presented. Sometimes they have special interest groups on jails who would be interested in sponsoring and developing these programs. If not, approach the executive secretary or an officer of the association to find out how to be included on the conference program. You can also use their membership mailing list and newsletter to publicize your conference program or workshop, as long as you start well in advance of the meeting.
5. Criminal justice institutes are university-based training facilities that receive federal money to provide continuing education and training for sheriffs. They have facilities as well as training staff, mechanisms for publicizing training within their geographic area, and are usually well known to jail personnel.
6. Library schools often provide some type of continuing education, have money and faculty for workshops, have publicity capability and facilities.
7. The National Institute of Corrections (NIC) currently has six regional jail centers throughout the United States. They have specialized resources, funding for workshops, and correctional trainers; high visibility with jail personnel; and publicity capability.

Use Appendix A for help in locating sponsors in your state. You can use form A, the Sponsors Worksheet, to list sponsors and their resources.

Planning Committee

The planning committee's five to seven members should effectively represent the sponsors, public librarians and jail staff with jail library programs, and jail staff and librarians without jail library programs. Be sure that the members have high visibility and credibility in corrections and librarianship and that they have extensive knowledge of their field and of fellow practitioners. The workshop coordinator is a member of the planning committee, as is the outside evaluator, if you have one. Depending on the type of workshop, you can also include former inmates and representatives from other

4 Planning the Workshop

Form A Sponsors Worksheet

| Name of Institution | Contact Person | Resources (Check those available) ||||||||
		Funds	Resource People	Publicity	Facilities	Local Arrangements	Workshop Coordinator	Newsletter
State Library Agency								
State Corrections Agency								
State Library Association								
State Corrections Association								
Library School								
Criminal Justice Institute								
NIC Jail Center								
Library System								
Local Jail								
Public Library								
Regional Library Association								

community agencies. To keep the planning committee small, look for individuals who can represent several groups, such as a sheriff with jail library service who is president of the state sheriffs association (one of your sponsors).

Major responsibilities of the planning committee frequently include:

1. Making sure that both jail personnel and librarians are involved in planning, conducting, and participating in the workshop (see pp. 10–11 for ideas)
2. Providing information on the present scope of jail library service in your state and on practitioners' needs
3. Providing assistance in selecting a general workshop approach through their knowledge of participants
4. Providing feedback on appropriate workshop content
5. Helping to select workshop length, location(s), and date(s) that will encourage attendance from both fields
6. Providing suggestions for resource people, speakers, and trainers
7. Suggesting effective publicity strategies
8. Suggesting funding sources and being involved in budget preparation.

When the workshop coordinator is a volunteer with no release time from work, some of the coordinator's tasks may be delegated to the planning committee members.

Before the first planning committee meeting, be sure that committee members have read *Jail Library Service* and the first section of this manual.

Workshop Timeline

The workshop coordinator can use this list of major workshop tasks to decide which tasks to do first, schedule activities, identify the person or group doing each task, and keep track of which tasks have been completed. This timeline is based on a two-day workshop. In reality some workshops may take longer than six months to prepare. A local workshop or a presentation at a meeting could be organized with less complexity in a shorter period of time. An asterisk denotes tasks generally delegated to the site coordinator.

Before the Workshop

SIX MONTHS

_____ Select sponsors, form planning committee, and hold first meeting.

_____ Conduct needs assessment (unless already done).

_____ Determine type of workshop.

_____ Develop workshop objectives.

_____ Develop budget.

_____ Assign responsibilities: workshop coordinator, members of planning committee.

_____ Design the workshop.

_____ Consult local, state, and national calendars for possible date conflicts, and determine date(s).

_____ Select major speaker(s) and confirm acceptance by mail. Request biographical data for publicity.

_____ Set maximum number of participants.

FIVE MONTHS

_____ Select site and confirm arrangements in writing.

_____ Determine deadline for registration.

_____ Send announcements to library and correctional newsletters.

_____ Notify selected national journals and associations.

_____ Make arrangements for printing and mailout of publicity flyers.

_____ Prepare workshop flyer.

_____ Select site coordinator and confirm.

_____ Decide on training techniques to use in workshop.

FOUR MONTHS

_____ *Arrange for necessary equipment.

_____ Continue working on workshop design.

_____ Select small group leaders and confirm.

THREE MONTHS

_____ Mail out/distribute workshop flyer and registration form.

_____ Set up preregistration procedures.

_____ File general outline and workshop budget with sponsor.

_____ Determine content of registration packet.

_____ Compile appropriate bibliographies and handouts.

_____ Double check with speakers concerning any visuals that may need to be produced or handouts to be printed.

_____ Begin gathering exhibit or display materials.

TWO MONTHS

_____ Make final arrangements for speakers' accommodations and travel.

_____ *Arrange for meals and coffee breaks.

_____ *Arrange for necessary directional signs to and at site.

_____ *Prepare information about housing, workshop location (map, if necessary), and parking to send to registrants.

_____ Design evaluation instrument based on objectives.

_____ *Select rooms for workshop and indicate room arrangement.

_____ *Prepare local information about restaurants, places to see, etc., for participants.

8 *Planning the Workshop*

ONE MONTH OR LESS

_____ Check all arrangements with site coordinator.

_____ Confirm registrations and forward any advance information or materials to participants.

_____ *Review all previous arrangements with a representative from your facility.

_____ *Confirm number of participants with facilities representative (for meal and seating arrangements).

_____ Be sure that handouts are printed and available at workshop location.

_____ *Prepare registration packets.

_____ *Compile registration list and make name tags for participants.

_____ Reconfirm date and responsibilities of speakers and small group leaders.

_____ Send prepared news releases to appropriate news media.

_____ *Double check arrangements for equipment.

_____ Check with everyone involved in planning to make sure all assignments have been completed and there are no last minute problems.

_____ *Set up displays.

During the Workshop

_____ Brief the speakers on the overall training design and answer questions about their presentations. Generally, the coordinator and the resource people meet the evening before the workshop begins.

_____ *Supervise participant registration and collect workshop fees.

_____ Coordinate the workshop as it is being conducted. If you do not want to be the moderator, you can select someone else.

_____ *Maintain liaison with facilities representative to ensure that all arrangements run smoothly during the workshop.

_____ Conduct feedback sessions during the workshop with speakers, consultants, and small group leaders to revise the workshop as needed, if your workshop lasts longer than one day.

_____ Conduct participant evaluation.

_____ Debrief immediately after the workshop with speakers, small group leaders, and the planning committee members on the strengths/weaknesses of the workshop and on participant evaluations.

After the Workshop

_____ Send thank-you notes to speakers, session leaders, site coordinator, facilities contact person.

_____ Pay bills and balance budget.

_____ Compile evaluation data and write the evaluation report. Report back to your planning committee and the sponsors. Send a copy of the workshop report (form D) to ASCLA for their file on training in jail library service.

_____ Provide follow-up assistance or information (or locate consultants who can) as requested by workshop participants.

_____ See that a six-month follow-up is conducted to ascertain progress in jail library service.

_____ Schedule final planning committee meeting to evaluate workshop and to make decisions about further training.

The Participants

Selecting Participant Groups

Participants should be drawn from the following groups:

1. Staff of jails and staff of public libraries with nearby correctional facilities, particularly those jail and library staff who will carry out, plan, or decide about introducing the service. In small libraries this may be the head librarian. In a medium-sized or large library this may be staff in the adult services department, outreach services department, books by mail program, bookmobile, or public services department. In small jails this might be the sheriff; in medium-sized jails, the jail manager or the staff members responsible for programming; in larger jails, perhaps a jail librarian.

2. Library system staff members and consultants. They can consult with libraries within their system and plan follow-up jail library service workshops.

Also, there is a trend among correctional institutions to close down small local jails and open larger jails for the populations of several counties, areas comparable in size to library systems. As this trend continues, jail library service may be carried out by a library system to a multicounty jail.

3. State correctional consultants and state library agency consultants, especially institutional or outreach consultants. They work with regional library systems and individual public libraries and jails and can provide follow-up workshops at local or state levels.

4. Community agencies serving local jails and their state counterparts, including adult education programs, colleges or universities with continuing education or CLEP course credit, mental health or social service agencies, employment counselors, parole officers, and agencies with community services directory or information and referral file.

5. Friends of the Library, library volunteers, library board members, library school and corrections students and faculty, librarians from other types of libraries, law librarians, members of interested civic groups, local city or county officials, librarians from public libraries whose communities contain no jail.

Once you have decided which of these groups of participants you will involve in your workshop, ask the planning committee to help make an estimate of workshop attendance or to set a limit on the number of participants.

Encouraging Participation by Sheriff-Librarian Teams

Encourage attendance by jail staff and librarians from the same community so that they can begin a plan for jail library service during the workshop. Your workshop will have more likelihood of producing new or improved service if jail and library staff come as planning teams. These groups traditionally get their training through different institutions, and budgets are not set up to handle different training approaches. Therefore, it will take special effort to get both groups to the same workshop. Here are some ideas to get you started.

1. Publicize adequately to both groups so that both librarians and sheriffs are notified about the workshop. You will need to use different publicity techniques to reach both groups (p. 24). The planning committee will be particularly helpful here.
2. Choose locations that are accessible, and consider holding workshops in more than one location to reach most jail and library staff.
3. Be sure to include in your workshop content areas of real interest to both jail staff and librarians.
4. Reimburse travel and expenses or part of expenses for participants. You might give priority to sheriffs or the sheriff-librarian team from the same community.
5. Hold a one-day preconference at the state sheriffs association an-

nual meeting. Librarians would be invited, particularly those involved in successful jail library programs.

6. Award CEUs (Continuing Education Units) to participants through a university or other continuing education provider. A CEU is a nationally recognized record of participation in professional education. One CEU equals ten contact hours. Training must be recognized by an institution that has been given the right to award CEUs. Contact your major state university's continuing education division for information about CEUs in your area.

7. Find out who conducts the continuing education for jail staffs in your state, and try to jointly sponsor a workshop with them or have training in jail library service included in the training already being provided for jail staffs. You could contact your state correctional agency, state jail inspector (if you have one), the criminal justice center in your state, or the NIC Jail Center.

8. Suggest that sheriffs experienced in jail library service or other jail programming encourage other sheriffs to attend.

Workshop Content

Assessing What Participants Need to Learn

What do library and jail personnel need to learn to improve jail library service? To answer that question you need information about existing jail library service programs—how widespread the service is and what kinds of services are being offered. You also need to know how interested practitioners are in learning more about this service. The following sections suggest methods you can use to gather and interpret this information.

Existing Sources of Information

Begin gathering statistics and information that already exist in published sources and through personal conversations. Find out about jail programs as well as jail library service in your workshop area.

Questions to Ask

1. Are any public libraries in the workshop area currently providing jail library service? Which libraries? Which jails? What type of service?

2. How many jails are within the geographic area of the workshop? What is the inmate population of these jails? What is the average length of stay?

Sources of Information
(See Appendix A)

1. State library agency, especially the public library outreach consultants and institutional consultants; library systems; *ASCLA Survey;* outreach or institutional roundtable of state library association

2. State jail inspector; state correctional agency; Law Enforcement Assistance Administration (LEAA) regional planning agency; criminal justice institute; *ACA Jail Directory*

3. What (if any) previous training has been provided on jail library service?

3. State library agency; library systems; state associations

4. What public libraries are providing outreach services of any kind? What type of outreach service to what target groups?

4. State library agency; library systems; state library association, particularly committees on outreach

5. What community services are provided in the jails?

5. *ACA Jail Directory*; state jail inspector (if any); state correctional agency

Informal Telephone Calls

If there are only a few libraries providing jail service, you can telephone them to find out if they are interested in workshops on improving or expanding jail services. In addition, you can identify the largest five or six jails without library service and their corresponding public libraries and call both to see if they are interested in a workshop. The information gained in this way can frequently help you determine the utility of a mail questionnaire as well.

Contacts with Correctional Consultants

State department of corrections staff or the state jail inspector will have information on training needs, training opportunities, and current continuing education programs for sheriffs and jail personnel. Some states have mandatory annual training programs in the corrections field.

Mail Questionnaire

If there is little or no available information about jail library service, use questionnaires to identify libraries and jails involved in library programs and to ascertain practitioner interest in a workshop. The questionnaire could be mailed by the state correctional agency or the state library agency, distributed at a state or regional conference, or included in a library system, state agency, or professional association newsletter.

Two sample forms have been provided. Form B can be sent to public libraries and jails to gather basic information about the existence of jail programs and library service. Form C can be used to gather more detailed information from jail librarians and public librarians currently providing jail library service.

Making Decisions Based on Findings

After gathering the data, the first question is whether or not to hold a workshop. Involve the planning committee in considering these questions:

1. Is there support for a workshop, either from practitioners or from a sponsoring group who puts priority on generating practitioner interest?

Form B Jail Library Service: A Questionnaire

To: Jails and public libraries

From: Workshop coordinator

We are planning a workshop on jail library service. Please help us provide training that will meet your needs by completing the following questionnaire and returning it to me by (date).

1. Name of person responding:_____

    Title:_____

    Name of institution:_____

    Address:_____
            Street   City   State   Zip

    Phone: (Area Code:_____)_____

2. Name of city/county jail (if different from #1):_____

    Name of sheriff/jail administrator:_____

    Address:_____
            Street   City   State   Zip

    Phone: (Area Code:_____)_____

3. Average daily number of inmates in jail:_____

    Average length of stay of inmates:_____

4. Is library service currently being provided to jail inmates?___ ___
                                                                             yes no

5. If no, are you interested in having library service available to inmates?

6. If yes, briefly describe service.
    ____Public library provides materials.
    ____Jail provides its own professional librarian.
    What services and materials are provided to inmates and staff?

7. What types of programs are available to the inmates? (Check ALL that apply.)
    ____Counseling   ____Vocational rehabilitation
    ____Education   ____Recreation
    ____Reentry   ____Religious services
    ____Other (describe)

8. If you do not have jail library service, would you be more interested in (check one):
    ____Half-day workshop on what jail library service is.
    ____One-day workshop on how to establish jail library service.

9. If your jail has library service, would you be interested in a workshop on how to expand your current program? ____yes ____no

    What topics would you like to see included?

Form C Jail Library Service: A Questionnaire

To: Jails and public libraries involved in jail library service

From: Workshop coordinator

We are planning a workshop on jail library service. Please help us provide training that will meet your needs by completing the following questionnaire and returning it to me by <u>(date)</u>.

1. Name of person responding:_____

    Title:_____

    Name of institution:_____

    Address:_____
              Street   City   State   Zip

    Phone: (Area Code:)_____

2. Please provide information about the jail/library with which you cooperate.

    Name of jail or library:_____

    Name of sheriff/librarian providing service:_____

    Address:_____
              Street   City   State   Zip

    Phone: (Area Code:)_____

3. Average daily number of inmates in jail:_____

    Average length of stay of inmates:_____

4. What types of programs are available to the inmates? (Check ALL that apply.)

    ____Counseling   ____Education   ____Vocational rehabilitation
    ____Reentry   ____Recreation   ____Religious services
    ____Other (describe)

5. Patterns of library service (Check ALL that apply):

    ____Permanent on-site collection   ____Delivery service of requests
        by public library   ____Bookmobile
    ____Rotating deposit collection   ____Other (Please specify)
        by public library
    ____Bookcart/bags to cells

6. Describe staff that delivers the service.

7. Hours per week of service: _____

8. Materials (Check ALL that apply):

    ____ Hardbound books   ____ Legal materials
    ____ Paperbacks   ____ Coping information
    ____ Magazines   ____ Educational materials
    ____ Newspapers   ____ Ethnic cultural materials
    ____ AV materials   ____ Other
         (please specify)   (please specify)

9. Describe your services.

10. What are the three most pressing problems you face with jail library service?

11. What are your future plans or hopes for improving library service to jails?

12. Are you interested in a workshop on expanding your current jail library service? ____ yes ____ no

    List the five topics you are most interested in:

Revised from a survey form used by ASCLA, Library Service to Prisoners Section.

2. Are there jails in your area where inmates stay more than three or four days?

If you plan to hold a workshop, you need to decide whether to provide an awareness of jail library service to those without such knowledge; information on beginning jail library service to those providing a minimal service or those with an interest in the service; or techniques for more extensive library programming to those providing basic service. In making this decision, consider what would potentially affect the largest number of inmates and what would meet the most immediate practitioner needs and interests.

Selecting a Workshop Section 2 of this manual includes details on conducting the following workshops. Review workshops that interest you, modify and combine techniques that meet your objectives, or decide to design your own workshop.

Books behind Bars Service

Increasing Awareness of Jail Library Service
(2–4 hours)

An introduction to jail library service that provides information and an opportunity for participants to explore and change their attitudes. This workshop can be used as a preconference or conference program, a system workshop, a staff development program for local jails and libraries, an introductory session of a two- or three-day workshop, or a beginning session in areas with jails that lack library service. Designed for those with little or no information or experience in jail library service, it can be used to evoke interest in longer, more intensive workshops, or can be modified for groups of librarians, groups of jail personnel, and groups with staff from both institutions.

Establishing Jail Library Service

Workshop for Public Librarians and Jail Personnel
(1½–2 days)

This workshop is a step-by-step approach to planning and starting jail library service, using *Jail Library Service* as a planning manual. During the workshop, participants will begin a plan for jail library service with input from jail personnel and former inmates and will know how to complete the plan when they get back to their communities. It can be most effectively used with sheriff-librarian planning teams from the same community. It can be used as a separate workshop or as a component of a longer workshop. It has been designed for those who wish to start jail library service or improve minimal service.

Jail Library Service Is More than Books

Using Community Resources to Expand Services
(1 day)

This workshop provides information about selecting and implementing services beyond basic book delivery to the jails—legal information, educational materials and courses, reentry information, group programming, and staff services. It can be used separately in an area where there are several established jail library programs or as the final component of a two- or three-day workshop. It has been designed for those who already have jail library service or who have attended "Establishing Jail Library Service." Community agency personnel are included in addition to jail and library staff.

Conference on Improving Jail Library Service

A State/Regional Perspective
(2–3 days)

This workshop is based on the National Institute on Library Service to Jail Populations. It provides presentations on various aspects of jail library service by state or regional library and correctional specialists. Appropriate as a statewide or multistate conference, it was designed for those who want information about the current state-of-the-art, trends, and issues in jail library service.

Workshop Combinations

These workshops can also be combined to produce a training series or a longer three-day workshop. A workshop series can be held with sessions one to three months apart in the following order: "Books behind Bars," "Establishing Jail Library Service," and "Jail Library Service Is More than Books." Participants can select which sessions to attend based on their training needs. The three-day workshop will contain a half-day for "Books behind Bars," one and one-half days for "Establishing Jail Library Service," and one day for "Jail Library Service Is More than Books." Participants can select which segments to attend. In this way, someone who knows nothing about jail library service can attend the entire three-day workshop and return home ready to implement services, especially if attending as part of a sheriff-librarian planning team. Those interested in only a basic level of service can stay for one or two days, while those already providing basic service can attend the last day only.

The Jail Library Game

A simulation
(2 hours)

In addition to these ideas, you might want to consider "The Jail Library Game," developed by the ASCLA Library Service to Prisoners section for its program at the 1978 American Library Association Conference in Chicago. The game has been particularly effective with groups of librarians. See Appendix B for a copy of this two-hour conference program.

Workshop Objectives

Since providing jail library service requires a mix of knowledge, skills, and attitudes, be sure that your objectives state clearly the information participants will gather, the skills they will learn, and the attitudes they will explore as a result of the workshop. Focus your objectives on what the participants will learn, rather than on what speakers will provide.

> Instead of: *The speakers will present information on the status of jail library service in the state.*
> Say: *The participants will identify three jail library service programs in their area.*

For examples that correspond to the workshop you're designing, see pages 33, 47–48, 76, and 81. These objectives are detailed so that the trainers can use them in designing the workshop and the workshop evaluation. You will need to modify these sample objectives based on the needs of the practitioners in your area.

If you need help in writing objectives, see:

> Robert F. Mager, *Preparing Instructional Objectives*, 2nd ed. (Fearon-Pitman, 1975).

During the workshop evaluation process, you will refer back to the workshop objectives to determine the extent to which the objectives have been met.

Designing the Workshop

Now that you know the type of workshop you are interested in and the specific objectives you want to accomplish, you are ready to design the content and techniques of the workshop. Turn to Section 2 of this manual. Read "Using the Workshop Designs" for general suggestions, and review the workshop design(s) that interest you most. Feel free to design your own workshop or add your ideas to suggested workshop designs. Plan to modify a workshop design or combine learning activities from different workshops to fit the needs of your practitioners, your own skills, and the available resource people.

Resource People and Trainers

Whoever is responsible for designing the workshop will be most heavily involved in locating workshop speakers. The planning committee will also be invaluable in suggesting excellent resource people and speakers in their state or region. Frequently resource people will be recommended to you by practitioners in whom you have confidence. No matter what the source of the recommendation, consider these questions as you select your speakers.

> Are they enthusiastic about jail library service?
> Do they know the content area?
> Are they good speakers and comfortable in front of an audience?
> Are they willing to spend the time needed to prepare adequately for a good presentation?
> Do they have the skills needed for your workshop, such as small group skills?
> Are you considering this person because he or she is a "big name" or because of qualifications?

Identifying Speakers

Here are ideas for resource people and how to find them. Consult Appendix A for additional information on agencies and organizations.

1. Sheriffs supportive of good jail library service programs. Recommendations can come from public librarians providing good jail library service and the state sheriffs association.
2. Librarians connected with good jail library service programs. Contact your state library agency, library systems, and participants and resource people at the National Institute.
3. Former inmates who used jail library service inside. Contact the Fortune Society and CONtact, Inc.
4. Correctional experts who know about ACA standards, the legal basis of jail library service, court orders, jail trends, and funding sources. Contact a criminal justice institute, state corrections agency, NIC Jail Center.
5. Library consultants, particularly institutional and outreach consultants who know the status of jail library service in the area, funding sources, standards. Contact your state library agency or library systems.
6. Public librarians familiar with service options and materials. Contact your state library agency and library systems and participants and resource people at the National Institute.
7. Correctional and library trainers, workshop leaders, and small group facilitators experienced in designing workshops and in using different training techniques (case study, role play, small group work). Contact trainers and small group leaders at the National Institute, state library agency consultants, criminal justice institute staff, and system consultants.

Working with Speakers

Be clear with speakers about your expectations, and give them complete information about the workshop. If possible, contact potential speakers by telephone, providing a short description of the workshop, their role, the dates, and an inquiry about fees (if appropriate). If they are interested, negotiate with them about the content of their presentation and exact fees.

After the initial telephone contact:

1. Send a letter of confirmation, specifically outlining time, place, and what is expected of them. Be sure to describe reimbursement procedures and the honorarium offered. Ask that any equipment or special aids be requested in writing.
2. Be sure that any preconference mailings and the final agenda are sent to all speakers and workshop leaders. Any advance information on the audience should also be sent.
3. Send speakers a copy of *Jail Library Service* and your workshop outline.
4. Arrange housing and transportation.
5. Request biographical information.

6. Call each speaker shortly before the meeting to confirm arrangements.
7. Arrange an informal meeting for all resource people before the program.
8. Before audiotaping or videotaping, secure the speakers' permission.
9. Prepare a backup plan in case a speaker cancels.
10. Send a letter after the workshop expressing your appreciation.

Workshop Evaluation

Look at your workshop objectives and design questions that will let you find out whether they have been met. Include questions that will measure participant learning of information, skills, and attitudes. To measure behavior change as a result of the workshop—which you cannot do at the workshop—design a follow-up questionnaire to see whether new and improved jail library programs have occurred.

There are a number of different types of evaluation that you will want to consider. A half-day workshop will require fewer evaluation techniques than a three-day conference. Here are some ideas:

Before the Workshop

During the planning process, have a member of the planning committee (not the workshop coordinator) or an outside evaluator provide feedback on how the planning for the workshop is proceeding. Is the planning committee functioning smoothly? Is the planning going according to schedule? Have participants been adequately informed about the workshop? What needs to be done to improve planning for the workshop?

During the Workshop

Do a short daily participant evaluation that is compiled and shared with workshop leaders and speakers each evening so that changes can be made during the workshop based on participant feedback. Share the results of these evaluation forms with participants the next morning.

Conduct a final workshop evaluation by participants, by the workshop coordinator, by speakers, small group leaders, and planning committee members at the conclusion of the workshop through evaluation forms, interviews, written reports, or verbal feedback. Sample evaluation forms are included with each workshop.

After the Workshop

You will be interested in how many jail library service programs are initiated or expanded following the workshop, since this is your ultimate goal. This will require follow-up with participants three to six months after the workshop. State library agency, state correctional agency, or library system consultants may be able to develop and distribute a questionnaire or do some on-site visits.

Outside Evaluator

To help with the evaluation of your workshop—particularly a lengthier workshop or a workshop series—you can select an outside evaluator. This person should not be involved in presenting the workshop and should have expertise in workshop design and training. A state library consultant, a criminal justice institute faculty member, or a correctional agency consultant might provide good choices.

Final Evaluation Report

After the workshop, you or the outside evaluator will be responsible for compiling the final evaluation results and writing a report on the workshop. Distribute copies of this report to sponsors, the planning committee, and other interested persons. Send a copy of form D to ASCLA for their file on training in jail library service. In this way groups interested in training can find out what has been done and who is active in their area. You can become a resource person for other groups wanting to conduct workshops.

Logistics

Workshop Length

Review the basic workshop designs on pages 16 and 17 to help you make a decision about the length of your workshop. What you want the participants to learn at the workshop will affect the length of the program. Providing basic information will take less time than expecting participants to write a plan for jail library service. Attitude change may take more time than describing a particular library program.

Also consider the amount of time that practitioners in both professions can be away from their work. Include travel time in decisions about scheduling the first session on the first day and the final session on the last day of the workshop. If you are limited to a certain amount of time, be reasonable about what participants can experience. These workshop designs are tightly scheduled to include the maximum number of activities.

Choosing Workshop Dates

First determine the dates to avoid. Your planning committee can be invaluable here. Find out if there are particularly busy times of the year for librarians or sheriffs in which meetings are not generally held. Find out about scheduled local, state, regional, and national correctional and library meetings. Check with the state library, library systems, and criminal justice institutes to find out about scheduled library and corrections workshops, training sessions, and university courses.

Once you have determined the times to avoid, you can then choose your tentative workshop dates, allowing three to six months to plan and arrange for the workshop. Check to make sure that the facilities and your key resource people will be available at the time you have selected.

Form D Jail Library Service: Workshop Report Form

Return to: ASCLA, American Library Association, 50 East Huron St., Chicago, IL 60611

1. Title of workshop:_____

2. Sponsor(s):_____

3. Location(s)/Date(s):_____

4. Number of participants:_____

5. Brief description of content and types of participants:_____
   _____
   _____

6. Attach a copy of the agenda or program.

7. Attach a list of participants.

8. Name of workshop coordinator:_____

   Institution_____ Position:_____

9. Major speakers

   Name   Position   Institution
   _____
   _____
   _____

10. Was the program videotaped?_____ Audiotaped?_____

11. Person involved in the design of the workshop who can be contacted for further information:

    Name:_____ Position:_____

    Institution:_____

    Mailing address:_____

    Work phone:_____

12. Name and address of person completing this form:

    _____
    _____
    _____

Deciding on Locations

There are many factors to consider when choosing a location:

1. Choose a site where librarians or jailers will be gathered for a professional conference or other kind of training.
2. Choose location(s) that are centrally located for participants. (For example, people should not be asked to drive more than one or two hours for a one-day session.)
3. Select locations that are easily accessible.
4. Look at where larger jails—the jails with the most inmates—are located. Choose locations within easy reach of jails that house a majority of the state's inmates. You may choose to hold the workshop in more than one location.
5. Consider replications of training in various locations throughout the state to reach sheriffs and public librarians from the same communities.
6. Be sure that you have a site coordinator at the location of your choice.
7. Choose a location with facilities adequate for the level of training planned and large enough for the number of anticipated participants.

Selecting Facilities

Different workshops need different facilities for displays, small group work, large meetings, and nearby jails that can be visited. See the workshop design in Section 2 for a description of the specific facilities you will need. Do not alter the training to fit the facilities; find facilities adequate for the training. There are many institutions that have facilities for meetings: public libraries with meeting rooms, criminal justice institutes at universities, library schools, universities with continuing education centers, and even hotels and motels. Frequently motels will offer free meeting rooms and reduced rates for participants' rooms.

Be sure to check the room(s) ahead of time, even if the facilities sound excellent, and even if they are located at some distance from you. They *must* be seen so that you can determine if the rooms are appropriate for your workshop and the size of your group. You will also need to note what you will have to bring with you on the day of the workshop.

For a detailed discussion of selecting facilities, see:

Ruth Warncke, *Planning Library Workshops and Institutes* (ALA, 1976), chapter 12.

Site Coordinator

Dealing with local arrangements is one of the most time-consuming aspects of holding a workshop. The workshop coordinator should delegate local arrangements, negotiations about workshop facilities, and participant registration to a site coordinator. The site coordinator should be a staff member from the jail or library in the community that is hosting the workshop, possibly someone associated with the facility.

Responsibilities of the site coordinator are asterisked in the Workshop Timeline (pp. 6–9). For a good discussion of the details involved in local arrangements, see:

> Ruth Warncke, *Planning Library Workshops and Institutes* (ALA, 1976), chapter 12.
> L. B. Hart and J. G. Schleicher, *A Conference and Workshop Planner's Manual* (AMACOM, 1979).

Publicity

Be sure to aim publicity at both public librarians and sheriffs. You need to use all possible strategies to reach your participants. Rely on your planning committee for advice on effective publicity methods. Be sure to publicize the workshop well in advance; three to six months is not too early. Some of the more common methods of publicizing workshops are:

1. *Announcements in library and correctional periodicals*. Get the publication deadlines from periodicals and newsletters so that the information can reach them on time. (See form E, Publicity Worksheet, for types of periodicals.)

2. *Direct mailout of publicity flyers*. Your mailing list should include public librarians in communities with jails and local sheriffs. Use the *American Library Directory*, the *ACA National Jail and Adult Detention Directory*, and the directory of jails in your state. Frequently state library and corrections agencies and library systems make mailing labels or mailing lists available. You can also locate mailing lists from professional associations, criminal justice institutes, and library schools.

3. *Direct telephone calls* to individuals you especially want to attend.

4. *Journal articles*. Before the workshop, ask the planning committee members to write articles on jail library service for the library association and state correctional association journals. The workshop can be mentioned in these articles. Be sure to get the publication deadline from the journals so that you can get the articles in print before the workshop.

Sample publicity materials can be found with the workshop designs.

Budgeting

A budget is a planning tool. It should list everything you think you will need for your workshop and identify possible categories of expenses. A budget is not meant to be restrictive, but rather is an aid to good planning. Do not assume you cannot plan an excellent workshop or include a needed item because of cost. Plan the workshop as you would like it to be, listing in the budget all the items and their costs. Be sure that the budget is complete and includes accurate cost figures. If the total is more than your available funds,

Form E Publicity Worksheet

Type of Periodical	Title	Contact Person	Publishing Deadline	Accepts Full-length Articles
State library agency newsletter				
State correctional agency newsletter				
Library system newsletter				
State library association newsletter				
Regional library association newsletter				
State corrections association newsletter				
State sheriffs association newsletter				
Criminal justice institute newsletter				
Library school newsletter				

you can look at alternative strategies, including increasing your funding or finding ways to get what you need at reduced or no cost.

Form F is a budget sheet that indicates types of expenses you can anticipate, cost ranges or how to determine costs, and alternate strategies for holding good workshops with limited funds.

Money for workshops can come from a variety of sources:

1. State library agencies have money for workshops, including grant funds.
2. Library systems.
3. State correctional agencies and criminal justice institutes.
4. State associations for conference programs and preconferences.
5. Sponsors will often be willing to provide in-kind services or pick up some of the expenses, as indicated in the budget sheet.
6. Grant proposal to request special funding from one of the above. You might want to write a grant proposal to pay for participant travel expenses, especially for sheriff-librarian teams and jail staff.
7. Workshop fees can subsidize all or part of the costs. Be careful not to discourage participation by charging too high a fee. Since you have worked so hard to involve both jail and library staff, check with the planning committee to see if a fee would discourage the attendance of one or both groups. Be sure to include the cost of *Jail Library Service* in the fee.

Form F Budget Worksheet

Budget Categories	Description	Cost	Alternate Funding Strategies
A. Consultants, trainers, resource persons, speakers	A. 1. Travel expenses A. 2. Expenses for food and motel/hotel	A. 1. Identify exact cost A. 2. $50-$75/day average	Consulting and teaching staff from various agencies often have expenses paid by agency: 1. State library agency 2. State correctional agency 3. Criminal justice institute 4. Library school 5. Library systems
B. Consultant fees	B. Pay for number of days at workshop, plus 1-2 days preparation if this seems reasonable	B. Fees range from $75-$200/day; $150/day average	Consultants from state libraries, public library systems, state correctional agencies usually do not charge fees. Public librarians and sheriffs might be willing to serve as resource people for expenses plus $50-$75/day.
C. Planning committee's expenses for their meetings	C. 1. Travel expenses C. 2. Expenses for food and motel/hotel	C. 1. Identify exact cost C. 2. $30-$65/day average	Planning committee members reimbursed by their own institutions or sponsor/cosponsors. This category includes costs incurred by workshop coordinator and site coordinator.
D. Travel and expenses for sheriffs and public librarians	D. Could be partial or complete reimbursement for some or all participants	D. Travel expenses for car, plane, etc. $40/day for food and motel/hotel	Possibility of grant money from state agencies or library systems. Give priority to librarian-sheriff planning teams from same community with larger jails. Check cost-benefit ratio of replications of workshop to reach target groups versus paying participant expenses to central location.
E. Secretarial/clerical help	E. Typing forms, correspondence, handouts, etc.	E. Get local costs from typing service	Try to get sponsors to provide secretarial support from their own staff.

(continued)

28 *Planning the Workshop*

Form F (cont.)

F. Publicity	F. 1. Printing announcements F. 2. Mailing announcements F. 3. Layout and design	State agencies, state associations, other cosponsors might be willing to absorb the cost of mailout and phone calls to their particular constituency.
G. Phone and mail	G. 1. Correspondence G. 2. Phone calls	Same as F above.
H. Materials	H. 1. *Jail Library Service* for each participant	Discount rates based on quantity State agencies purchase for participants Participants purchase copy during registration
	H. 2. Workshop handouts--agenda, worksheets, evaluation	Sponsors--professional association, state agency, public library system, criminal justice institute--might be able to absorb printing cost or print them for you.
	H. 3. Rental of nonprint media	Sources of media (producers and distributors) might provide free of charge to reach group of potential buyers or for public relations.
I. Facilities	I. Meeting rooms	Usually cosponsor supplies use of rooms. Motel/hotel supply free when participants are staying there.
J. Equipment rental	J. Projectors, screens, tape recorders, etc.	Facilities may be able to provide free. State agency or professional association may be able to loan or pay for.
K. Refreshments	K. Coffee, juice, soft drinks for breaks	Sometimes sponsors will pay. Participants can pay for what they want.
L. Registration materials and workshop supplies	L. Packets, badges, paper, newsprint, etc.	Sometimes host institution will supply registration badges and packets free. Sponsor may supply workshop supplies.

Additional cells:
- H. 1. Purchase from ALA
- H. 2. Get printing costs
- H. 3. $20-$30 per film average cost
- I. Check to see if there is charge
- J. Find out what equipment is available at the facility and its cost
- K. Get cost from host institution
- L. Get cost
- F. 1. Get printing costs
- F. 2. Figure postage costs
- F. 3. Get layout costs

# Section 2

Conducting the Workshop

Using the Workshop Designs

This section includes four different approaches to conducting jail library service workshops. Since no one ever does a workshop exactly like anyone else, our assumption is that these workshops will be changed—content added, handouts modified, activities deleted, new techniques designed. But our purpose is to provide examples that you can modify. These workshops are very tightly scheduled to provide a variety of techniques. You may want to delete some activities that are of less interest in your area to allow participants more time for discussion and consultation with speakers and each other.

The first two workshops are very detailed, providing enough information for less experienced trainers to use them as is or to modify them with little difficulty. These designs include goals and objectives, indication of target groups and resource people, publicity materials, agenda, suggested procedures, evaluation methodology, and a complete set of handouts for conducting the workshops. The last two designs contain suggestions for designing your own workshops. Content of the workshops is based on *Jail Library Service,* which can be used as a participant workbook or text. See Appendix B, "The Jail Library Game," a simulated experience that has been used successfully with groups of librarians.

The training designs incorporate a variety of active learning techniques so that participants can be involved in and take responsibility for their own learning—small group brainstorming, problem solving, and planning sessions; individual/team work sessions; minilectures; role plays; and before-workshop assignments. As you decide on training activities, keep these points in mind:

1. Use a variety of techniques that involve participants actively in their own learning.
2. Keep lectures to a minimum, and balance with small group discussion or individual/team work sessions.
3. Give the participants adequate opportunity to apply the information to their situation.

4. Give participants time to talk to resource people and share skills and problems with other participants.
5. Be sure that information presented applies to your state or region. The status of jails and jail library service varies from state to state.
6. Be sure that librarians, jail staff, and ex-offenders have a chance to work together and to practice joint problem solving and decision making.
7. Be flexible and modify your agenda during the workshop if participants feel they need more time to work on service plans or to consult with resource people and each other.
8. Use nonprint materials, jail tours, role play, or simulation to allow librarians to experience the realities of working in a jail in a low-risk situation.

Materials

This manual lists or includes all materials needed for conducting a jail library service workshop, using *Jail Library Service* as the basic participant workbook and resource for trainers. Participants can read *Jail Library Service* before, during, or after the workshop. Trainers can use *Jail Library Service* as a source for developing their minilectures.

The first two workshop designs include additional handouts:

    Publicity materials
    Preregistration form
    Agenda
    Various handouts and worksheets (found at the end of the workshop design)
    Role plays, case studies, and discussion starters
    Evaluation forms (found at the end of the workshop design)

You may reproduce worksheets and handouts in this manual without further permission from the publisher. You can also use some of the forms as models for developing your own forms. Directions for each workshop indicate which handouts need to be modified, which need to be compiled, and which can be photocopied as is.

Training Techniques

Small group activities allow participants to explore their feelings, discuss different approaches, get a chance to practice communication skills, and do joint decision making with other professional groups—in short, active and immediate involvement. For any but a very short small group activity (5–10 minutes), a small group facilitator should be part of the group. The facilitator will not usually be one of the participants but one of the resource people or a trainer with small group skills. The facilitator reviews directions for group activities, helps keep the group focused on its tasks, and sees to it that all members have a chance to participate. However, the facilitator should not do the group's work for it, nor try to dominate group activities with his or her own perspective. The small group facilitator should see that group members have a chance to get acquainted before beginning small group tasks.

Brainstorming is one specific small group technique that is used to identify as many ideas, possible solutions to a problem, or participant reactions as possible within a short period of time (usually 5–10 minutes). No evaluation or questioning of ideas is allowed. One group member records all ideas on newsprint for the group to consider at a later time. Later, the group can evaluate the responses, synthesize the most workable ideas, and come up with a recommended approach or solution.

Role plays have been included as optional activities in some of the workshop designs. They provide participants the chance to practice real-life behavior in low-risk situations to see what happens. Role play is a valuable learning strategy in jail library service workshops. However, with groups of people from different fields it is especially important that the facilitator conducting the role play be comfortable with this technique.

Nonprint materials provide factual information in a form that provides realism and emotional impact. However, do not assume that a film is always better than a speaker. Preview all nonprint materials before you decide to use them, and be sure that the content and treatment are suitable for your audience and your objectives. See Appendix C for a list of pertinent nonprint materials.

Less experienced trainers will want to consult the following books for more information on selecting and using different training techniques.

> Larry Davis, *Planning, Conducting, Evaluating Workshops* (Learning Concepts, 1974).
> Martha Jane Zachert, *Simulation Teaching of Library Administration* (Bowker, 1975).

Books behind Bars

Introduction

Setting and Length
Sessions are usually two or three hours, generally held in conjunction with other programs or meetings, such as a program at an annual association conference or a library system meeting. This session would be appropriate for a staff development activity for jail and library staff in the same community. It can also be shortened for an orientation session on jail library service for community groups, library board members, Friends of the Library groups, student groups, local officials.

Number of Participants
Any number of participants can be accommodated.

Target Audience
Jail personnel and public librarians with varying degrees of interest in and information about jail library service are the primary groups. Some sheriffs may come only because jail library service is required in the American Correctional Association standards and because of court orders. Public librarians may have some experience with outreach services to other groups but may never have been inside a jail. Participants may not be convinced that jail library service will work in their communities. This workshop is designed for a group containing both librarians and jail personnel, with suggestions for adapting it for a group of librarians and a group of jail personnel.

Workshop Methods
The success of this workshop rests heavily on the sheriff-librarian team leading the workshop and on how they interact with each other and with the participants. The session includes small group activities to encourage communication among participants. If you need a shorter two-hour session or if you are unable to arrange the room to enable participants to work together in small groups, you can delete the small group activities marked with an asterisk.

Room Arrangement and Facilities
For a large group, participants can be seated in an auditorium, in rows of chairs, or around tables. Participants need to be able to move chairs to form small groups of seven to ten people if the optional small group activities are used, or they can talk with people sitting near them if they are seated in an auditorium.

Resource Persons
1. Resource persons can include a sheriff-librarian team who have set up a successful jail library service program together, or a sheriff and a public

librarian from different communities who are involved with jail library service and can work together to present the program. It is absolutely essential that both a librarian and a sheriff or jail administrator present the information and work with the group—even though the group may be solely librarians or solely jail personnel. It is important for the group to realize that the service must have the backing and expertise of both librarians and jail staff. Having both present the workshop is a powerful way to communicate this.

2. A correctional consultant knowledgeable in standards, security problems, correctional procedures, and credible to sheriffs can also be used successfully.

Workshop Goal

This workshop will introduce jail personnel and public librarians to the idea of jail library service and will provide information and a chance to express fears and prejudices so that participants are willing to consider providing such a service.

Workshop Objectives

1. Jail personnel and librarians will have positive feelings about working with each other.
2. Jail personnel and librarians will be interested in jail library service.
3. Jail personnel and librarians will realize that jail library service is feasible in their own communities and that it benefits inmates, jail staff, public library staff, and the entire community.
4. Jail personnel and librarians will gain the following information:
   a) Jail library service is an integral part of American Correctional Association standards, state jail standards, and court orders.
   b) The American Correctional Association and the American Library Association have indicated that public libraries are to provide jail library service and that jail administrators do not have to fund and manage their own libraries by themselves.
   c) Resource people and consultants are available in their own states to help them start library service.
   d) Jail staff provide excellent security while librarians work in the jail.
   e) Library service is best provided by the library through the use of its staff and/or trained volunteers.
   f) The library is responsible for equal access to information for all inmates.
   g) Library service is available to jail staff as well as to inmates.
   h) Different levels and options for jail library service exist.
5. Participants will begin to investigate the possibility of jail library service in their local communities after the conference program.
6. Participants will use *Jail Library Service* after the conference program for further information on how to begin jail library service.

Form G   **Sample Publicity Flyer**

Books Behind Bars

A Conference Program

FOR JAIL PERSONNEL
AND LIBRARIANS

April 15, 198X
9 A.M.-12 noon
Hilton Hotel, Green Room

Come for answers to the following questions:

- What are the benefits of library service to inmates and jail staff?
- How can you comply with the legal requirements for jail library service?
- How can you provide library service to jail inmates in the face of budget and staff limitations?
- What problems will you face with library service inside?
- What materials and services do inmates want?
- Where can you get help in setting up your program?

Sponsor: Outreach Services Roundtable,
         State Library Association

Speakers:

Jane Brown, Jail Librarian   Mark French, Sheriff
Smithville Public Library   Smith County Jail

Form H **Sample Agenda**

Books behind Bars

April 15, 198X, 9 A.M.–12 noon

Agenda

9:00– 9:10	Introduction of speakers
9:10– 9:20	Participant introductions
9:20– 9:45	What is jail library service?
9:45–10:05	Problems of jail library service
10:05–10:20	Reaction to problems
10:20–10:35	Break
10:35–11:10	Breaking stereotypes
11:10–11:30	Advantages of jail library service
11:30–11:50	How to get started
11:50–12 noon	Evaluation of program

Individual consultations with speakers after the program

Jane Brown, Jail Librarian
Smithville Public Library
118 West Main
Smithville, KS 66803

Mark French, Sheriff
Smith County Jail
904 Oak
Smithville, KS 66803

Sponsored by: Outreach Services Roundtable, State Library Association

Workshop Design 9–9:10 INTRODUCTION 10 minutes
Materials: Agenda

Content: The team welcomes the group and introduces themselves, briefly discusses the agenda, and makes the following points:

1. Interest in jail library service is spreading rapidly.
2. There is a legal mandate for jail library service.
3. Public libraries are interested in expanding user groups, maintaining public support, justifying their budgets. Public libraries are experienced in providing service to institutions in the community—nursing homes, hospitals, etc.
4. Jail library service can happen anywhere there is a jail and a public library—any size jail and any size public library. It can start with little or no additional funds and staff and will increase as funds and additional staff are available.

9:10–9:25 PARTICIPANT INTRODUCTIONS 15 minutes
Content: The team asks the following questions of the group as a whole:

1. Who are the jail staff? Librarians? What other groups are here?
2. How many are from jails with less than 50 inmates? Between 50 and 200? More than 200 inmates?
3. How many are currently providing jail library service?

Optional content: The team divides large group into smaller groups of seven to ten people based on the size of the inmate population of the jails. Be sure that each group has public librarians and jail staff. If small groups are not formed, participants talk to the people sitting near them.

9:25–9:45 WHAT IS JAIL LIBRARY SERVICE? 20 minutes
Purpose: To provide an overview of the topic

Materials: Nonprint materials, if available, especially slides showing library service in jails

Content (*Jail Library Service,* chapters 1, 5–7): The team provides the following information:

1. Examples of different types of library service in different sizes of jails
2. Pertinent standards and court orders
3. Status of jails and jail library service in the state
4. Jail security procedures
5. What sheriffs need to know before librarians start providing library service

a) Librarians support the right to information—and inmates will be one of their user groups with this right.

b) Library service is not to be used as a reward and punishment system.

c) Library materials and information are not to be censored, except in such cases as books about making bombs, escape from jail.

d) Repeat positive note that public libraries are community agencies able to supply library service.

9:45–10:05   NEGATIVE REACTIONS TO   20 minutes
             JAIL LIBRARY SERVICE

Purpose: To allow participants to state problem areas, so that discussion about different approaches is possible.

Presentation technique: Panel of two or three public librarians and two or three sheriffs air their negative feelings and hesitations about jail library service in front of the large group.

1. The team encourages the audience to participate, keeps the negative feelings coming, and does not comment on problems that are raised: "Any more problems?" or "We really found that one hard, but what was even harder was. . . ."
2. Librarian team member keeps track of librarians' feelings on newsprint, and sheriff team member keeps track of jail staff members' feelings.

Optional presentation technique (to replace the previous one): Each small group lists fears of sheriffs and fears of librarians on two sheets of newsprint. Small groups take turns reading one fear for each group until all fears are shared with the large group.

Materials: Newsprint and magic markers; overhead projector or chalkboard, if desired

Content: Typical fears and prejudices of sheriffs include:

1. Prisoners can't read. Why bring them books?
2. You want to coddle the inmates. They don't deserve it.
3. Inmates will use books to start fires, clog up toilets, smuggle in dope.
4. They'll lose or destroy books, and we don't want to have to pay for the books.
5. Library service would jeopardize security. We can't have outsiders in the jail.
6. We don't want women inside the jail.
7. Hell, no one brings me and the other jail staff things to read.

Typical fears and prejudices of librarians include:
1. It is safe? I don't want to work inside a jail.
2. Do I have to go in the cell with the prisoners?
3. Catcalls—How will I feel as the only woman inside?
4. I'm frightened about being with accused/convicted felons.
5. They'll lose or destroy my books.

10:05–10:20   RESPONSE TO NEGATIVE FEELINGS   15 minutes

Purpose: To identify possible approaches for solving problems

Content:
1. The team stresses that all programs started out with questions and fears. But there are now x number of jail libraries in the state/region, and many of these are working to provide additional services to meet standards and court orders. How can this kind of service exist in the face of so many problems? Librarians and sheriffs work together to make it happen.
2. The team gives examples of the major problems they worked through to provide library service to inmates.

Optional presentation technique (to replace some of the above discussion of problems by the team): Each small group brainstorms solutions to one of the problems previously identified. Ideas can be shared with the entire group.

10:20–10:35   BREAK   15 minutes

10:35–11:10   BREAKING STEREOTYPES   35 minutes

Purpose: To provide time for librarians and jail personnel to communicate with each other

Presentation technique:
1. Form groups made up only of sheriffs and only of librarians. Each group brainstorms about their ideas of jails and their ideas of libraries.
2. Groups share their perceptions of each other and themselves.

Materials: Newsprint and magic markers for each group

Optional presentation technique (that can be used in addition to or instead of the previous technique):
1. Sheriffs help librarians to approach the sheriff in their local community about jail library service. Sheriffs can role play the librarians' approach. Librarians can play sheriffs.

2. Librarians help sheriffs to approach the library staff in their community about jail library service. Librarians can role play the sheriffs' approach, and sheriffs can play librarians.
3. Each small group writes on newsprint a list of tips on approaching sheriffs and tips on approaching librarians. These ideas can be shared verbally or by posting the newsprint on the wall.

11:10–11:30   WHO GETS WHAT OUT OF   20 minutes
JAIL LIBRARY SERVICE?

Purpose: To discuss the benefits of service to everyone involved

Content: The team makes the following points:

1. Jails meet legal requirements and standards; library services are geared to jail staff as well as inmates; inmates who have things to do are less likely to cause trouble, rather than being bored and restless.
2. Inmates get a chance to use time spent in jail to prepare for time after release so that they are less likely to return to jail; inmates have options for beneficial use of time in jail.
3. Librarians provide service to another community group; increase community support; increase budget justification.

Optional presentation technique (to replace previous technique): Small groups brainstorm advantages of jail library service and write these on newsprint. The team summarizes for the group as a whole.

11:30–11:50   JAIL LIBRARY SERVICE CAN HAPPEN   20 minutes
Purpose: To encourage interest after the program

Materials: Jail Library Service; forms I and J

Content:
1. The team discusses the use of *Jail Library Service.*
2. The team discusses available resources.
3. The team discusses what steps participants can take in their communities.

11:50–12   PARTICIPANT EVALUATION   10 minutes
OF PROGRAM
Materials: Forms K and L.

Individuals can consult team members with questions as time permits.

For Jail Staff Only

To modify the "Books behind Bars" workshop for use with jail personnel only, you will need to bring in two to four librarians supportive of and experienced in jail library service, in addition to the sheriff-librarian team. During the program, you will want to be sure to emphasize the following points:

1. ACA standards, court orders, legal requirements, state standards require that jails provide library service to inmates. Libraries can support the jail in meeting other ACA standards pertaining to programming that are not directly involved with library service.
2. Jail staff can have library service brought into their jail by working with the public library in their community.
3. Here's what library service means in the jail: examples of services, samples of different kinds of materials, kinds of information and reference/research services available. (Provide good descriptions.)
4. Emphasize library service to jail staff. They should get the same kind of library service as inmates—recreational reading, educational materials, reference questions answered, newspapers and magazines, as well as correctional materials and journals.
5. The sheriff team member should emphasize that librarians can do far more than a jail staff member delivering books once a week. Emphasize the librarian's role in talking directly to inmates and jail staff about their reading and informational and educational interests.

For Librarians Only

To modify the "Books behind Bars" workshop for use with librarians only, you will need to bring in two to four sheriffs supportive of jail library service, in addition to the sheriff-librarian team. In the description of jail library service (9:25–9:45), you might want to make the following points:

1. Jail provides a captive audience of nonusers.
2. Court mandates are a reality. Sheriffs and jails are being sued; they know they need to provide library service, but they do not know how to do it. ACA standards require jails to have library service.
3. ALA resolution says that public libraries are responsible for serving jails.
4. The library can start with what is possible with no increase in budget or staff and continue to expand as support grows.
5. Jail library service and the increasing involvement of different community agencies in the jails are trends.
6. This is a service you can do easily from any size of public library because you are reaching out to a group who has no service; anything you do is important.
7. Describe how the library can meet inmate needs and needs of jail staff. Do not sentimentalize the plight of the inmate because you do not want to polarize librarians against sheriff and jail staff.

Materials

The following are materials needed for this workshop:
1. *Jail Library Service* includes the basic information to be presented at the workshop. Copies should be available to all participants—probably for purchase.
2. Nonprint materials, if desired (Appendix C), and appropriate equipment.
3. Supplies: name tags; newsprint, magic markers, masking tape; overhead transparencies and overhead projector or chalkboard (if preferred).
4. Handouts to be compiled: "Jail Library Service: Who to Contact" (form I).
5. Sample handouts to be modified: "Agenda" (form H).
6. Handouts ready to copy: "Jail Library Service: What to Do in Your Local Community" (form J); Evaluation Form (form K); "Request for Further Information" (form L).

Form I   Jail Library Service: Who to Contact

Directions: Use this sheet as a guide to compile a handout for participants. Include the name, address, and telephone number for each of the following groups and individuals in your state or region. Indicate which ones have funds available.

1. State library institutional consultant
   a) Ask about the availability of Library Services and Construction Act (LSCA) funds.
   b) Ask about state jail standards. Do they include mention of jail library service?
   c) Make copies of jail library standards for your state if they exist.

2. State correctional agency consultant or planner
   a) Ask about Law Enforcement Assistance Administration (LEAA) funds.
   b) Ask if there is a state jail inspector. List his or her name.

3. National Institute of Corrections (NIC) regional model jail. List the nearest one (Appendix A).
4. State correctional association
5. State sheriffs association
6. Pertinent groups within the state library association (public libraries section, outreach services group, institutional services group). Give name of contact person.
7. Libraries serving jails in your state and the name of contact person
8. Ex-offender groups
9. Participants and resource people at the National Institute on Library Service to Jail Populations. Get this list from ASCLA.

Form J Jail Library Service: What to Do in Your Local Community

Directions: Here are some things you might do when you get home to begin planning for jail library service. Check those activities you want to do, and make notes under each as to your timetable, who you will contact, and how you will go about doing it.

____1. If you are a librarian, talk to other library staff and see if they are interested in starting jail library service.

____2. If you are a jail administrator, talk to other jail staff and community services personnel inside the jail about the advantages of jail library service.

____3. Talk to the jail administrator or the library director about his or her interest in jail library service.

____4. If you are a librarian, tour your local jail and find out how many inmates are there.

____5. Read *Jail Library Service* for further ideas. Share the guide with other staff.

____6. Get more information from state library consultants, public library system consultants, or libraries and jails already providing the service.

____7. Talk to the library board, the Friends of the Library, the county commissioners or city manager, and other community groups for support.

____8. Form a planning group of librarians and jail staff to begin planning the service.

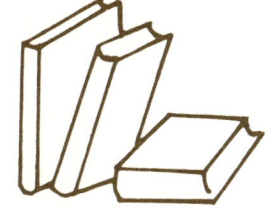

Form K Evaluation Form

Job Category

____Public library director
____Public library staff member
____Jail administrator
____Jail staff member
____State library consultant
____Library system consultant
____Correctional consultant
____Other _____

Size

____Number of inmates
____Population of community

Experience

____Currently providing jail library service
____No jail library service

1. Before you came to this session, what was your interest in jail library service?

    no interest   1   2   3   4   5   very interested

2. Now what is your interest in jail library service?

    no interest   1   2   3   4   5   very interested

3. If you are a librarian, how comfortable do you feel about contacting your local jail administrator?

    uncomfortable 1   2   3   4   5   very comfortable

4. If you are a sheriff, how comfortable do you feel with the idea of library service in your jail?

    uncomfortable 1   2   3   4   5   very comfortable

5. Do you intend to begin planning for library service in your jail? ____ yes   ____ no   If no, why not?

6. Do you intend to read *Jail Library Service*? ____yes   ____no

7. Will you have your staff read *Jail Library Service*? ____yes   ____no

8. Would you be interested in a workshop on how to begin jail library service? ____ yes   ____ no

    What length of workshop do you prefer? ____ ____ ____
                                           1 day 2 days 3 days

9. List three steps you intend to take in your local community to begin planning for jail library service.

10. Additional comments about the workshop (use back of this sheet):

Form L Jail Library Service: Request for Further Information

To: State library institutional consultant/state correctional consultant

From: Name: _____

Position: _____

Library or Jail: _____

Mailing address: _____

_____

_____

Work phone: _____

Please send me the following information and materials:

Establishing Jail Library Service

Introduction

Setting and Length

This is a two-day workshop that can be held as a preconference of an association meeting or as a separate state or regional workshop sponsored by a state library and/or a correctional agency or an association.

Number of Participants

Participants should number 40 to 60, divided into small groups of seven to eight persons.

Target Audience

1. Sheriff-librarian planning teams from the same community, as well as sheriffs and public librarians from different communities who are interested in jail library service.
2. Library and jail staff who have already started a basic service and want to expand or get feedback on their current service.
3. State library and regional system consultants and correctional consultants who want to increase their consulting skills in this area.

Many participants will already be committed to jail library service and will want information on how to begin. Others will have some level of interest but will have questions needing answers before beginning service.

Workshop Methods

This workshop is based on presentations by different speakers, small groups working on actual plans for jail library service, role play and brainstorming to develop communication skills, and participant access to consultants to assist them with their plans of service. The content of the workshop is based on *Jail Library Service*. Worksheets and sample materials used during the workshop are found in *Jail Library Service*.

Room Arrangement and Facilities

During this workshop participants need to sit at tables in groups of six to eight people for the small group work. You will also need display space for six to eight tables of materials.

Resource Persons

The workshop involves a number of resource persons. Some may be taken from the participants if they happen to have special expertise in different areas of jail library service. Some resource persons will give short presentations on a specific content area; they will also be available to consult individually with participants.

1. Public librarian-sheriff team with successful jail library experience as workshop leaders and coordinators.
2. Additional public librarians and sheriffs who are involved in jail library service in different sizes of jails and with expertise in different services—legal, education, reentry, recreation, and staff services. Public library outreach staff and jail programming staff can be substituted, as well as state library consultants for outreach and institutional services and correctional consultants.
3. Former inmates (at least one for each small group).
4. Representatives from funding sources within the state (optional).
5. Small group facilitators (one for each small group) to assist small groups with communication exercises and jail service plans. Consultants from the library and corrections field can be used, as well as practitioners with some experience in working with small groups.

Workshop Goal

At the end of the workshop, participants will have begun a service plan for jail library service and will know how to complete it when they get back to their communities and can work with library and jail staff there.

Workshop Objectives

1. Librarians will learn about jail security regulations and procedures; will understand their responsibilities in following all security regulations without deviation; and will learn about other jail policies.

2. Sheriffs will understand the library's responsibility for the inmate's right to information; will find out about different library service options, including service to jail staff; and will learn about library policies.

3. Both sheriffs and librarians will receive specific information about jails and public libraries in their geographic region, about the status of jail library service in their state, about funding sources, and about consultant services and professional associations in the jail and library fields.

4. Participants will learn and practice planning and negotiating skills in groups made up of public librarians, sheriffs, and former inmates so that after the workshop participants can establish planning groups made up of jail and library staff members and inmates and can provide library service to jail staff and inmates.

5. Participants will begin preliminary plans for initiating/expanding jail library service for their local community, involving joint planning by librarians and jail staff. These plans will demonstrate that participants know how to:

   a) Gather information and statistics about pertinent library and community resources.
   b) Identify techniques for assessing the informational needs of inmates and jail staff on a continuing basis.
   c) Develop service objectives.

d) List possible delivery modes.
e) Generate a variety of needed services.
f) Identify pertinent types of materials.
g) Identify key policy areas that need to be negotiated with jail administrators and library directors.
h) Indicate areas to be covered in a service contract.
i) Procedures for evaluating the service.

6. Participants will learn how to promote jail library service to library staff, to inmates, to jail staff, and to the community.

7. Participants will receive individualized technical assistance on their service plans from library and correctional consultants during the workshop and will contact consultants within three months after the workshop as additional questions arise in revising and implementing their service plan.

8. Participants will learn how to use *Jail Library Service* in further planning, implementation, and staff training within their local communities.

9. Participants will begin or expand some type of jail library service within six months after the workshop.

Preregistration Materials

Before the workshop, you will want to send a number of items to people who will be attending. This will give participants a chance to find out about their local jail or library before the workshop, and it may encourage their jail administrator or librarian to come with them as part of a planning team. Workshop planners will also want to make sure that the workshop content matches participants' expectations and that they know a little about participants' jail and library situations.

To find out about participants, mail the preregistration form (form N) with the publicity brochure (form M). Participants will mail this back to the workshop coordinator before the workshop.

To encourage participants to find out about their local jail and local library, send the following planning forms to be filled in before the workshop:

1. "Gathering Information about Your Jail" (form Q)—librarian can visit the jail and meet the sheriff; sheriff can bring information.

2. "Gathering Information about Your Library" (form R)—sheriff can visit the library and meet the librarian; librarian can bring information.

You may also decide to send *Jail Library Service* before the workshop (if this is included in the registration fee or being provided free by workshop sponsors). Since the workshop will be a concentrated experience, participants may be interested in reading *Jail Library Service* ahead of time, particularly chapters 1, 3, 5–7.

Form M Sample Publicity Flyer

ESTABLISHING JAIL LIBRARY SERVICE
WORKSHOP FOR PUBLIC LIBRARIANS AND JAIL ADMINISTRATORS

Agenda

March 10	8:00- 9:00 A.M.	Registration
	9:00-11:45 A.M.	Overview of jail library service
	1:00- 2:15 P.M.	The librarian, the sheriff, the inmate
	2:15- 4:00 P.M.	How to work together
	7:00- 9:00 P.M.	Services and materials
March 11	9:00-10:15 A.M.	Assessing needs and locating funds
	10:30-12 noon	Writing a service plan
	1:00- 2:00 P.M.	
	2:00- 3:30 P.M.	Presenting the service plan
	3:30- 4:00 P.M.	How to locate additional help

Workshop Design: This workshop will include presentations by resource persons and small group work so that by the end of the workshop participants will have a plan developed to initiate or improve jail library service in their own communities. Teams of two or three library personnel and jail staff from the same community are encouraged so that planning can be more effective. Participants will receive a copy of a planning manual as part of their registration fee: **Jail Library Service**.

Registration and Fees: To preregister, complete the enclosed form and return to your state library by Feb. 20, 198X. You will receive further information about the workshop and some planning forms to complete and bring with you to the workshop.

Workshop fee: $25 per person, which includes a copy of **Jail Library Service**
Fees are payable the first day of the workshop

Sponsors: State Library
State Sheriffs Association
State Criminal Justice Institute

Resource People: List and indicate affiliation

Planning Committee Members: List and indicate affiliation

Place: Fort Scott Model Jail, Fort Scott, Kans.

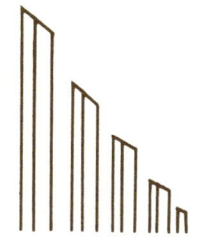

Form N Preregistration Form

Establishing Jail Library Service March 10-11, 198X
 Fort Scott Model Jail

Name:_____ Position:_____

Institution or Agency:_____

Mailing Address:_____

Work Phone:_____

1. Are you or have you been involved in jail library service?
   ____ yes   ____ no   Please describe:

2. Is the library currently providing service to the local jail?
   ____ yes   ____ no   Please describe:

3. If there is no jail library service, has the library ever contacted the local jail? Has the local jail ever contacted the library? With what results?

4. How many inmates are in the local jail?

5. Do you have special skills or experiences in jail library service that you would like to share? Please describe:

6. What other outreach services does the public library provide? List and describe briefly.

7. What types of community service programs does the jail provide to inmates? List and describe briefly.

8. Are you coming as a member of a planning team? List the other team members.

9. To help us conduct a workshop that better meets your needs, please rank the following topics in order of importance to you (1=most important; 7=least important).

   ____Designing adequate security

   ____Gaining the support and cooperation of others (jail personnel, library staff, inmates)

   ____Scheduling the service

   ____Determining the interest level and information needs of the jail population

   ____Legal requirements for jail library service

   ____Planning and implementing a program of library service

   ____How library service fits with programming needs

   ____Service options for jail service

   ____Selection of materials and formats

   ____Sources of funds and technical assistance

   ____Publicizing service to inmates, staff, and the community

10. List other topics you would like to learn about.

Return to:

Form O Sample Workshop Announcement

December 1, 198X

From: Barbara Mann
      State Library

"Establishing Jail Library Service" is the theme of a two-day workshop for public librarians and jail administrators and staff to be held on March 10-11, 198X, at the Fort Scott Model Jail, Fort Scott, Kansas. The workshop is jointly sponsored by the State Library, the State Sheriffs Association, and the Criminal Justice Institute.

Sessions will focus on:
- How to establish or improve jail library service
- Benefits of library service to inmates and jail staff
- How jails can comply with correctional standards and court orders
- How jail and library staff can work together to plan and provide programming
- Types of services and materials that inmates and jail staff want: educational, reentry, legal, recreational

Teams of two or three jail and library staff members from the same community are encouraged. Participants will develop a plan of jail library service for their own communities during the workshop.

Workshop coordinators are Margaret Sims, Jail Librarian, Smithville Public Library, and Jim Brown, Sheriff, Smith County Jail. Speakers will include representatives from funding sources, the state jail inspector, a law librarian and former inmates.

For more information and registration materials, contact: Barbara Mann, State Library, Box 1234, Topeka, KS 66801. Preregistration deadline--Feb. 20, 198X.

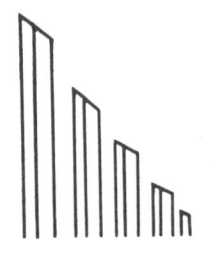

Form P **Sample Memo**

Feb. 1, 198X

To: Participants registered for the workshop on "Establishing Jail Library Service"

From: Barbara Mann, Workshop Coordinator

RE: Upcoming workshop

Welcome to the workshop on "Establishing Jail Library Service." I'm pleased that you have chosen to attend and look forward to meeting you and working with you during and after the workshop.

To get you off to a good start on planning library service for your local jail, I'm enclosing two worksheets that you need to fill in before you arrive at the workshop—one calling for information about your local public library and the other calling for information about your local jail.

If you have not met your library director or your sheriff, this is a good opportunity to find out about their facilities and services. Maybe you can suggest that they attend the workshop with you as part of a planning team from your community. If you have already decided to attend as a team, you can fill in these worksheets together.

There are several motels with restaurants within walking distance of the Fort Scott Model Jail, and all have agreed to give discount rates for workshop participants:

   Ramada Inn, 348 West Main, Fort Scott, KS 66609   888-444-5555

   Howard Johnson, 195 Elm, Fort Scott, KS 66609   888-999-8888

   Blazing Star Motel, 455 West Main, Fort Scott, KS 66609
      888-444-6789

The Fort Scott Model Jail is located at 544 West Main. A map of Fort Scott showing the location of the jail and the motels is enclosed. Free parking is available across the street from the jail.

If you have any questions, don't hesitate to contact me.

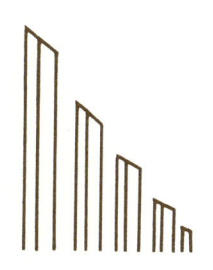

Form Q Gathering Information about Your Jail

Jail:_____ City:_____

Administrator:_____

Person providing information:_____ Position:_____

1. *Inmates*
    Current number_____   Average daily population_____
    Rate of turnover_____
    Ethnic groups   % Blacks_____   % Chicanos_____
                    % Other non-Anglos_____
    Women_____   Trustees_____
    Educational level (average)_____

2. *Security procedures*
    Attach a written list of security regulations to this form.

3. *Jail staff*
    Current number_____
    Administrators_____ Jail Staff_____ Other_____
    Describe the various staff positions and duties and the lines of authority within the jail. Indicate who reports to whom.

4. *Jail facilities*
    Which of the following options best describes the kind of space available in the jail for library use or storage:
    ____Extra room for library   Comments:
    ____Extra room for deposit collection
    ____Shelves in office
    ____Space in cupboard
    ____Other (describe)

5. *Jail budget*
    Does the jail have any money for library service or equipment?
    ____Jail budget   ____Inmate welfare fund   ____Other
    Comments:

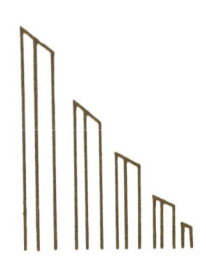

6. *Community services inside the jail*
   Indicate specific agencies and organizations for each category of service, and briefly describe the nature of their program inside the jail.
   Social services:

   Adult education classes:

   Medical services:

   Counseling services:

   Religious groups:

   Volunteers:

   Other groups:

7. *Schedule of services*
   Attach a written schedule of all of the above services provided and the jail's daily routines (meals, medical care, visiting hours, etc.)

8. Assess the level of interest in jail library service on the part of the jail. Were any problems mentioned?

Form R Gathering Information about Your Library

Library:_____ City:_____

Library director:_____

Person supplying information:_____ Position:_____

1. *Public library services to community*
   ____Deposit collections in community   Comments:
   ____Bookmobile services
   ____Adult education programs
   ____Film programs
   ____Book discussion groups
   ____Legal referral services
   ____Information and referral
   ____Other outreach programs
        (describe)

2. *Library materials*
   Check materials that could be made available in the jail. For these items, indicate whether the library could provide from its own collection (LIB) or whether the library could purchase (PUR).

   ____Paperback books   ____Legal books
   ____Magazines   ____Educational materials
   ____Newspapers   ____Ethnic materials
   ____Hardback books   ____High-interest/low-reading level
   ____Fiction   ____Foreign language books
   ____Nonfiction   ____Pamphlets, brochures, community
   ____Reference materials   materials
   ____Records, audiotapes   ____Pictures, posters
   ____Films   ____Other_____

3. *Library staff*
   Indicate which of the following might be possibilities for staffing the jail library service project.

   ____Professional librarian, full-time
   ____Professional librarian, part-time
   ____Paraprofessional librarian (full- or part-time)
   ____Volunteer trained by librarian
   ____Other_____

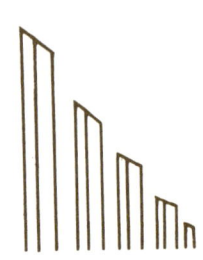

4. *Library budget*

   Does the library have any money for library service, materials, or equipment?

   ____Library budget   ____Donations from community
   ____Grant proposal   ____Other_____
   ____Friends of the Library
   Comments:

5. Assess the level of interest in jail library service on the part of the public library.
   Were any problems mentioned?

Form S Sample Agenda

Establishing Jail Library Service
March 10-11, 198X

Agenda

March 10	8:00- 9:00 A.M.	Registration
	9:00- 9:25 A.M.	Introductions
	9:25- 9:45 A.M.	What is jail library service?
	9:45-10:30 A.M.	Problems
	10:30-10:45 A.M.	Break
	10:45-11:45 A.M.	Problem solving
	11:45- 1:00 P.M.	Lunch
	1:00- 2:15 P.M.	The librarian, the jail manager, the inmate
	2:15- 2:45 P.M.	How to communicate for joint planning
	2:45- 3:00 P.M.	Break
	3:00- 4:00 P.M.	How to communicate to promote the service
	7:00- 9:00 P.M.	Services and materials
March 11	9:00- 9:30 A.M.	Assessing needs and feasibilities
	9:30-10:15 A.M.	Funding possibilities
	10:15-10:30 A.M.	Break
	10:30-12 noon	Writing a service plan
	12:00- 1:00 P.M.	Lunch
	1:00- 2:00 P.M.	Writing a service plan
	2:00- 3:30 P.M.	Presenting the service plan
	3:30- 4:00 P.M.	Additional sources of help
	4:00 P.M.	Evaluation of workshop

Margaret Sims, Jail Librarian
Smithville Public Library
218 West Main
Smithville, KS 66803

Jim Brown, Sheriff
Smith County Jail
904 Oak
Smithville, KS 66803

Sponsored by: State Library   State Sheriffs Association

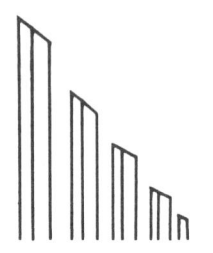

Criminal Justice Institute

Workshop Design

BEFORE THE WORKSHOP

Registration: Before the workshop, assign participants to small groups based on the size of their local jail. Try to have one sheriff or jail staff member in each group. State library consultants, library system staff, and correctional consultants can be assigned to groups as needed to balance the size. Groups should contain from six to eight people. Designate the group on the participants' name tags.

Tour of local jail (optional): If the local jail where the workshop is held is one of the NIC area resource jails or if it provides library or other types of programs, participants might be interested in a tour of the facilities, particularly participants who have never been inside a jail. Tours can be scheduled before, during, or after the workshop.

FIRST DAY

9–9:10   INTRODUCTION TO THE WORKSHOP   10 minutes
Materials: Agenda (form S)

Content: The team welcomes the group, introduces themselves, and briefly discusses the agenda.

9:10–9:25   PARTICIPANT INTRODUCTIONS   15 minutes
Content:
1. The team asks the following questions of the large group:
   a) Who are jail staff? Who are librarians? What other groups are here?
   b) How many are from jails with less than 50 inmates? Between 50 and 200? Over 200 inmates?
   c) How many are currently providing jail library service?
2. Participants introduce themselves within their small group and tell what three things they want to find out during the workshop.

9:25–9:45   WHAT IS JAIL LIBRARY SERVICE?   20 minutes
Purpose: To provide an overview of the service

Materials: Optional 16mm film or slides of jail library service (Appendix C) for part of presentation

Content (*Jail Library Service,* chapter 1): The team provides the following information to the large group:
1. Various service options and delivery modes for jail library service. Make the point that if you have a jail and a public library, you can start jail library service. Start with what is possible. This workshop will help you determine what is possible.

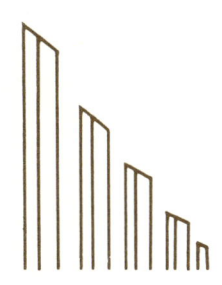

2. Legal basis of service—ACA standards, state jail standards, ALA resolution, court orders in the state.
3. Benefits/reasons for service for the jail, the inmates, the public library, and the community. Jail library service is surprisingly easy and has positive outcomes.
4. Status of jail library service in the state.
5. How the library can assist jail to meet ACA standards in programming areas other than library service.

9:45–10:05 NEGATIVE REACTIONS TO   20 minutes
            JAIL LIBRARY SERVICE

Purpose: To provide an outlet for fears and discomfort in the group so that possible approaches can be discussed.

Presentation technique:

1. Each small group brainstorms fears and negative reactions toward jail library service on newsprint—one sheet for librarians' fears and one sheet for sheriffs' fears.
2. Each group reads negative reactions until all fears are shared with the large group. Groups are careful not to duplicate responses already given.
3. Team lists negative feelings, encourages the flow of negative reactions, and does not provide solutions or comments to problems that are raised: "Any more problems?" or "We really found that one hard, but what was even harder was. . . ."

Materials: Newsprint and magic markers; blank overhead transparencies and overhead projector

Content: Typical fears and prejudices of sheriffs include:

1. Prisoners can't read. Why bring them books?
2. You want to coddle the inmates. They don't deserve it.
3. Inmates will use books to start fires, clog up toilets, smuggle in dope.
4. They'll lose or destroy books, and we don't want to have to pay for them.
5. Library service would jeopardize security. We can't have outsiders in jails.
6. We don't want women inside the jail.
7. Hell, no one brings me and the other jail staff things to read.

Typical fears and prejudices of librarians:

1. Is it safe? I don't want to work inside a jail.
2. Do I have to go in the cell with the prisoners?
3. Catcalls—How will I feel as the only woman inside?

4. I'm frightened about being with accused/convicted felons.
5. They'll lose or destroy my books.

10:05–10:30 RESPONSES TO NEGATIVE FEELINGS   25 minutes
Purpose: To begin to address some of the fears and negative feelings

Content:

1. The team stresses that all programs started with questions and fears. But there are now x number of jail libraries in the state, and many are working to provide additional services to meet standards and court orders. How can this kind of service exist in the face of so many problems? Librarians and sheriffs are here to work together to solve these problems.
2. The team provides examples of the major problems they worked through to provide library service to inmates and involves participants in suggesting solutions for different problems. Problems generated need to be explored fully as long as there are unresolved questions. This may mean extending the amount of time allotted.

10:30–10:45 BREAK   15 minutes

10:45–11:45 PROBLEM SOLVING FOR   1 hour
JAIL LIBRARY SERVICE
Purpose: To provide practice in problem-solving skills and communication between jail personnel and librarians

Content:

1. Small groups choose two or three problems and brainstorm possible solutions. Record ideas on newsprint.
2. Group evaluates possible solutions and decides on most practical solution.
3. The group discusses as many problems as time permits.

11:45–1 LUNCH   1 hour, 15 minutes

1–2:15 THE WORLD OF THE LIBRARIAN,   1 hour, 15 minutes
THE WORLD OF THE SHERIFF,
THE WORLD OF THE INMATE
Purpose: To provide insight into the different realities of jail staff, librarians, and inmates and their different roles in jail library service

Content:

1. The sheriff discusses what it is like in jail for the librarian.

a) Security rules and regulations and the reality of scheduling; what situations need to be reported to the sheriff
b) Getting along with other jail staff and working with inmates—feelings of discomfort, being the only woman, safety, clothing, what to expect
c) How to ask for help; who to ask for help when problems arise

2. The librarian indicates what it is like for the sheriff to have a librarian inside the jail.
   a) Basis of librarians' approach is freedom of information.
   b) Types and variety of materials—legal, reference, educational, fiction and nonfiction, newspapers and magazines, paperbacks, reentry brochures, staff services
   c) Importance of reference interviewing and reader's advisory service; importance of librarian for this service; and importance of time for librarian to talk to inmates during each visit

3. An ex-inmate discusses what it is like having library service and being inside.
   a) Inmate characteristics, emphasizing wide diversity of needs and interests
   b) Inmates' needs for different types of materials, services, and information
   c) How to work with inmates. Role play between librarian and ex-inmate to illustrate typical problems

Situation 1: The new librarian has trouble understanding inmates' street language and different culture. The librarian feels confused and somewhat intimidated.

Situation 2: An inmate desperately needs legal information for an upcoming court case and has a two-day deadline. The librarian promises to get this information but is inundated with other work and does not follow up. The inmate is angry—and now has lost a chance for a rehearing of his case.

Situation 3: A naive librarian acts friendly and pleasant and does not realize that an inmate's interest in her is a "con" to get favors for special library privileges or to cover up his attempts to rip off library materials.

2:15–4   HOW TO WORK TOGETHER   1 hour, 45 minutes
          TO PLAN SERVICE
Purpose: To provide practice in communication skills between librarians and jail personnel

Presentation technique: Combination of minilectures to large group and small group role plays for practice

Content:
1. Specialist in small group skills indicates importance of small group skills and of negotiation skills in planning and carrying out library service within another institution.
2. Small groups role play an initial meeting between the sheriff and the librarian.
    a) Divide small group members into teams of three—a librarian, a sheriff, and an observer. You might try role reversal. Have a librarian play the sheriff and a sheriff play the librarian ("Jail Library Game: Questions for Sheriffs to Ask" in Appendix B).
    b) Role play the librarian approaching the sheriff about the possibility for beginning jail library service. Role plays should last no more than 10 to 15 minutes.
    c) After the role play, role players dicuss their reactions, and observers provide feedback on communication techniques that seemed to work and those that were not successful. The small group facilitator leads the discussion.
    d) Optional activity: Workshop leader asks observers to share with the large group what techniques were most/least successful.

2:45–3 BREAK 15 minutes

3–4 HOW TO WORK TOGETHER
TO PLAN SERVICE (cont.)
Content:
1. Workshop leader indicates elements of successful negotiation.
    a) Know your bottom line.
    b) Know your situation and pertinent local information.
    c) Know your priorities.
    d) Know what you would like, in increasing levels of priority.
    e) Respect the other person's dignity, humanity, and their right to their own opinion, even if it is different from yours.
2. Participants resume small group role plays, as before. Groups choose two of the following situations as time permits.
    a) Librarian approaching hesitant library staff who do not want to serve "criminals."
    b) Library staff member approaching library director who is not especially interested in outreach services ("Jail Library Game: Administrator's Checklist" in Appendix B).

64 *Conducting the Workshop*

      c) Sheriff approaching jail staff who think library service will be too much trouble and who do not want a woman in the jail.
      d) Librarian and sheriff approaching mayor, library board, county commissioners who do not think inmates have a right to library service—and besides inmates cannot read.
      e) Librarian-sheriff team presenting idea to other community groups who do not understand or have inaccurate information about jail library service. For example, they think that a library would have to be built inside the jail, that it would be unsafe for a woman to work inside, that the cost of jail library service is prohibitive.
      f) Librarian trying to promote library service to apathetic inmates.

4:00   DAILY REACTION FORM
Participants indicate their reactions to the first day of the workshop by filling in the short evaluation form before leaving the small groups (form T).

4–7   BREAK FOR SUPPER
Workshop leaders and small group facilitators review Daily Reaction Forms and revise the remainder of workshop as necessary.

7–9 P.M.   SERVICES AND MATERIALS FOR   2 hours
JAIL LIBRARY SERVICE
Purpose: To provide information on available services and materials

Content (*Jail Library Service,* chapters 5–7)
1. Participants should have read *Jail Library Service,* chapters 5–7, before this session.
2. Participants will be gathering information for their own service plans to be written the following day.
3. Experienced practitioners discuss the following (10 minutes each):
    a) Legal materials and services (law librarian)
    b) Educational materials and services (librarian or adult educator who has taught inside)
    c) Reentry materials and services (public librarian, counselor, or other agency staff members working with ex-inmates)
    d) In-jail programs (librarian providing such programs)

e) Popular reading materials and nonprint materials (librarian)

f) Services for jail staff (librarian, state library institutional consultant, or sheriff)

4. Participants consult informally with experienced practitioners and with each other.
5. Displays of library materials are set up for the following areas: legal, leisure reading and nonprint, reentry, educational, staff services.

    a) A bibliography of the titles and a list of key publishers will be available for each display.

    b) Display materials may be acquired by contacting publishers (see *Jail Library Service,* chapter 6) or from libraries.

SECOND DAY

9:00 A.M. WRITING A PLAN FOR JAIL LIBRARY SERVICE — 3 hours

Purpose: To begin developing a plan for jail library service that involves jail and library personnel and ex-inmates

Presentation technique: Minilectures, followed by small group work to fill in planning worksheets on the particular topics

Materials: Worksheets in *Jail Library Service* as indicated; forms Q and R

Content (Jail Library Service, chapters 3, 4, 9)

9–9:30
1. Team quickly reviews information needed for planning specific library service.

    a) ACA and state jail standards
    b) Determining service needs (*Jail Library Service,* chapter 4)
    c) Reviewing present jail capability (form Q)
    d) Reviewing present library capability (form R)

9:30–10:15
2. Funding sources within the state (*Jail Library Service,* chapter 9)

    a) Panel of resource persons each speaking five to ten minutes and making available handouts on their particular funding source.
    b) Resource people on funding will be available to consult with participants individually after break as they work on their service plans.

10:15–10:30 BREAK — 15 minutes

Form T Daily Reaction Form

Date:_____

Circle one:

Content of Sessions 1   2   3   4   5   6   7
                    Outstanding   Inferior

Method of
Presentation   1   2   3   4   5   6   7
                    Outstanding   Inferior

What did you particularly like about today's activities?

What did you think could be improved?

Do you feel you need more information on any of the topics covered?

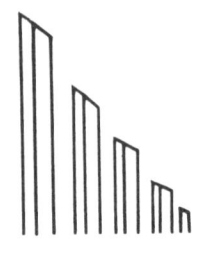

10:30–12   3. Within each small group, participants decide on what services and delivery mode to plan for. Ex-inmates should be included in the small groups.
   a) Team indicates that basic services should include those required to meet ACA and state jail standards:
   (i) Materials in general subject areas of interest
   (ii) Filling requests for specific materials
   (iii) Sources of current information—magazines and newspapers
   (iv) Filling reference and information requests
   (v) Policy on legal questions
   (vi) Information about community services and resources
   (vii) Materials for jail staff
   b) In small groups, participants write plan of service. Teams from the same community work together to produce one plan.
   (i) Small group facilitator briefs group members on different components of the plan, particularly writing objectives.
   (ii) Participants develop plan by filling in worksheets in *Jail Library Service* (pp. 18–20, 39–40, 52, 71, 81): service objectives, description of service, staffing, scheduling, delivery mode, materials, budget.

12–1   LUNCH   1 hour

1–2   CONTINUE WORKING ON SERVICE PLAN   1 hour
Participants discuss their plans with other group members, consultants, speakers, as desired.

2–3:30   PRESENTING THE SERVICE PLAN   1 hour, 30 minutes
Purpose: To allow participants to practice presenting their plans and to receive feedback on them.

Materials: Form U

Content:

1. Teams or individuals present their plan to a "library director" and "sheriff" (experienced librarian and sheriff) and an ex-inmate.
2. Consultants fill in feedback sheets and award points for different components of the plan.
3. If there are questions or additional matters to be worked out, participants continue to work, finding another consultant, other planning teams, etc.

Form U Plan for Jail Library Service Feedback Sheet

Name of Team:_____

Names of Consultants:_____

Directions: Rate each component of the plan by noting points earned. Provide comments and suggestions for improvement.

____1. Service objectives (significant impact; measurable; realistic)
(20 points)

____2. Description of service (adequate to meet needs; possible; well thought out; agreeable to both jail and library)   (20 points)

____3. Staffing (adequate to provide service well; evidence of training component for both library and jail staff; library staff allowed inside jail)   (15 points)

____4. Scheduling (appropriate for jail, library, and inmates' needs; realistic; security considerations)   (5 points)

____5. Delivery mode (appropriate for service and jail facilities)
(10 points)

____6. Materials (represent diversity of needs; current; for jail staff as well as inmates)   (15 points)

____7. Budget (adequate to provide service; represents joint contributions by jail and library)   (15 points)

4. As participants get their plans accepted, they can become members of existing consultant teams and assist in evaluating other plans.

3:30–3:45   IMPLEMENTING THE SERVICE   15 minutes
Purpose: To point out other pertinent information in *Jail Library Service*

Content: Team briefly identifies pertinent content in *Jail Library Service.*
1. Evaluation
2. Service contracts
3. Policy statements
4. Staff training
5. Reporting procedures
6. Promoting the service inside and outside the jail

3:45–4   WHO CAN HELP?   15 minutes
Purpose: To remind participants that they may have many resources to draw upon once they return home

Materials: Form I; list of participants; list of resource persons from workshop

Content: Team reminds participants of the people and groups able to help them begin jail library service.

4 P.M.   PARTICIPANT EVALUATION
Materials: Forms V, W, and X

Materials

The following are materials needed for this workshop:

1. *Jail Library Service* for each participant. This can be mailed to participants before the workshop, if desired. Many of the worksheets used during the workshop are included in *Jail Library Service.*
2. Nonprint materials may be substituted for some of the presentations or used for additional impact. Slides of actual jail library service would be useful (Appendix C).
3. Supplies: name tags; newsprint, magic markers, masking tape; overhead transparencies and overhead projector or chalkboard (if preferred); signs to designate small groups and display areas.
4. Handouts to be compiled: list of workshop participants, speakers, small group leaders with addresses and positions; funding sources in the state or region; state information on jails, public libraries, jail library service; "Jail Library Service: Who to Contact" (form I); bibliographies of display materials.

5. Sample handouts to be modified: Agenda (form S).
6. Handouts ready to copy: Daily Reaction Form (form T); "Report on Plan for Jail Library Service" (form V); "Plan for Jail Library Service Feedback Sheet" (form U); Evaluation Form (form W).

Form V Report on Plan for Jail Library Service

You may enclose a copy of the plan you (or your team) prepared during the workshop, or you can use this short report form. Please complete and return by the end of the workshop.

Name_____ Location:_____
 or
Team_____ Size of jail:_____

The service as designed is: ____a basic/beginning service
                             ____an expansion of present service
                             ____a new service

It is based on: ____needs assessment
                             ____interest survey
                             ____other

Please comment:

The tentative plan for service is (describe briefly):

Outline steps necessary before service can begin:

Groups/resources to contact:

Possible date for start up:

Any further comments:

Thank you.

Form W Evaluation Form

Please identify yourself according to the following categories:

Job Category

____Public library director
____Public library staff member
____Jail administrator
____Jail staff member
____State library consultant
____Library system consultant
____Correctional consultant
____Library trustee
____Other_____

Size

____Number of inmates in jail
____Population of community

Experience

____Currently involved in jail library service
____No jail library service

1. What do you think you will have to do first to begin or expand service to jails in your community?

2. Please list any program topics you felt were:
   a. Unnecessary
   b. Not covered sufficiently
   c. Not covered at all

3. Do you feel you had sufficient time to exchange ideas with the other participants?

4. Did you have sufficient time to consult with the resource people?

5. What session of the workshop was most useful to you? Why?

6. Workshop Activities
   a. Please comment on the presentations (use the back of this page if you need more room).
   Speaker   Content   Delivery

   b. Please comment on the small group work.

   c. Please comment on the workshop materials and displays.

   d. Please comment on the guide *Jail Library Service*.

7. If you were asked to redesign the workshop, what changes would you make?

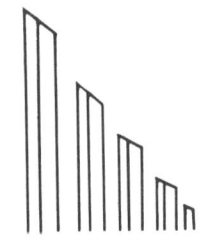

8. In the workshop preregistration form, you were asked to rank the following topics in order of importance to you.

Having attended the workshop, would you still place them in the same order?

Please rerank (1=most important; 7=least important)

*After each topic, place the letter that best describes your reaction to each session: V=very useful; U=useful; S=somewhat useful; N=not useful.

____Designing adequate security   ____*

____Gaining the support and cooperation of others (jail personnel, library staff, inmates)   ____

____Scheduling the service   ____

____Determining the interest level and information needs of the jail population   ____

____Legal requirements for jail library service   ____

____Planning and implementing a program of library service   ____

____How library service fits with programming needs   ____

____Service options for jail service   ____

____Selection of materials and formats   ____

____Sources of funds and technical assistance   ____

____Publicizing service to inmates, staff, and the community   ____

9. Please comment on your overall reaction to the workshop.

Form X Jail Library Service: Request for Further Information and Training

To: State library institutional consultant/correctional agency consultant

From: Name_____

Position:_____

Library or Jail:_____

Mailing address:_____

_____

Work phone:_____

1. Please send me the following information and/or materials.

2. I/other members of my staff would be interested in additional training/workshops. ____ yes ____ no

Please indicate specific content areas.

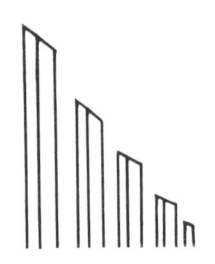

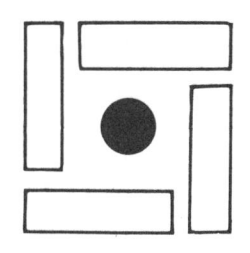

Jail Library Service Is More than Books

Introduction

Setting and Length

This is a one-day workshop that can be held by itself, as an optional third day of the "Establishing Jail Library Service" workshop, or as a follow-up workshop three to six months after the "Establishing Jail Library Service" workshop. This can also be held as a preconference or postconference at a professional association meeting.

Number of Participants

Up to 40 to 60 participants, divided into small groups of eight to ten based on the type of specialized service they are planning.

Target Audience

1. Public librarians and sheriffs who already have some basic library service established in their jails
2. Library systems that want to support jail library service
3. Community agencies and groups who are interested in cooperative services and programming with the jail and the public library: adult education, employment centers, vocational rehabilitation, probation/parole officers, social services, mental health programs, and community colleges or universities with continuing education or nontraditional education programs

Teams of public library staff, jail staff, and community agency staff from the same community should be encouraged.

Workshop Methods

This workshop is based on presentations by different speakers, small groups developing plans for specialized services, and participant access to consultants to assist them with their service plans. The information in this workshop goes beyond what is found in *Jail Library Service*. Displays of materials supporting the specialized services should be available.

Resource Persons

This workshop involves the use of a number of resource persons. Some may be taken from the participants if they happen to have special expertise in different specialized areas of jail library service. Resource persons will give short presentations and will serve as small group leaders for participants who are planning services in their area of expertise. The workshop coordinator can be a jail librarian, a state library institutional consultant, or a consultant knowledgeable in specialized jail programs.

Resource persons can include:

1. Public librarians and jail staff who have implemented different

types of specialized services and can function as small group leaders
2. Ex-inmates who can speak of the need for such services
3. Representatives of community/state agencies (education, employment, social services, etc.)
4. Representatives of funding sources (LSCA, LEAA, NEH, state agencies, local fund raising, local budget increases)
5. State library consultants for outreach and institutional services, library system consultants, and correctional consultants

Workshop Goal

This workshop will increase the awareness of jail personnel, public librarians, and community agency staff for expanding jail library service by doing joint programming and will provide experience in selecting and planning for one specialized service. By the end of the workshop, participants will have begun a written plan for a new specialized service in their jail based on cooperative planning with another community group.

Workshop Objectives

1. Participants will find out about available specialized service options—adult education, community information and referral services, group programming, reentry skills and coping information, legal materials and services, staff services.
2. Participants will learn how to assess inmate interest and possible community resources to support specialized service.
3. Participants will become familiar with specialized materials to support these services.
4. Participants will identify key community groups and agencies to involve in planning specialized services.
5. Participants will explore support from regional library systems—interlibrary loan, consultation, training, special collections of materials, actual provision of jail library service.
6. Participants will find out about available sources of funds at local, state, national levels: foundations, LSCA, LEAA, NEH, local fund raising, increased library and jail budgets.
7. Public librarians, jail staff, ex-inmates, and staff from other community agencies will learn how to work together to plan more specialized services for jail inmates and jail personnel.
8. Participants will begin planning one specialized service in conjunction with jail staff, former inmates, and other community agencies that they can begin to implement in their local situation.
9. Participants will receive individualized technical assistance on their plan of service during the workshop and will contact consultants within three months of the workshop during revision and implementation of the plan.
10. Participants will expand jail library service to include some type of specialized service within six months after the workshop.

Form Y Sample Agenda

Jail Library Service Is More than Books
March 10, 198X

Agenda

8:00- 8:30 A.M.	Registration
8:30- 8:45 A.M.	Introductions
8:45- 9:45 A.M.	What are specialized jail library services?
9:45-10:30 A.M.	Expanding services with community agencies
10:30-10:45 A.M.	Break
10:45-12 noon	Selecting a specialized service
12:00- 1:00 P.M.	Lunch
1:00- 3:00 P.M.	Planning specialized library service
3:00- 3:15 P.M.	Break
3:15- 5:00 P.M.	Presentation of plan
5:00- 5:15 P.M.	Wrap-up and evaluation

Workshop Coordinator: Barbara Mann, Institutional Consultant
State Library

Cosponsors: State Library   State Dept. of Corrections

State Dept. of Education

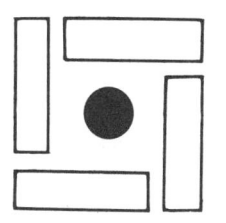

Workshop Ideas

You can modify many of the techniques and handouts from the "Establishing Jail Library Service" workshop to plan this workshop on expanding jail library service. Use activities from the second day of the "Establishing Jail Library Service" workshop if you want to provide time for participants to begin their plans for specialized services.

Here are some specific ideas for the morning sessions:

WHAT ARE SPECIALIZED   1 hour
JAIL LIBRARY SERVICES?

1. Workshop leader discusses rationale for specialized services (*Jail Library Service*, chapters 6–7; *ACA Manual of Standards for Adult Local Detention Facilities*)
    a) Jail standards call for additional community services for inmates, and libraries can support such services.
    b) Inmate needs that are still unmet.
    c) Public library wants to expand its role to cooperate with other community agencies and groups in many of its programming efforts to avoid duplication of services, better use of community funds, and stronger programs.
    d) Trend for cooperation and coordination of community services.
    e) Library provides services and materials to other community agencies and groups in support of their community programs.
2. Public librarians and jail staff with specialized services talk about the programs, emphasizing particular community agencies they are cooperating with. Speakers each have ten minutes and point out pertinent ACA standards.
    a) Adult education at varying levels
    b) Reentry/community information and referral
    c) Legal services
    d) Staff services
    e) Group programming

EXPANDING SPECIALIZED SERVICES   45 minutes
WITH COMMUNITY AGENCIES

Panel of jail staff member, librarian, ex-inmate, and community agency personnel react to case studies. They brainstorm ideas on the types of services that each agency could provide and how these services could be coordinated, with input from participants.

Case Study #1: 75 percent of the inmates of the Johnson County Jail do not have a high school diploma. Of these inmates, about 50 percent stay in the jail for six months or longer. The jail is an older facility with inadequate lighting and no space for inmates to attend classes in the jail or to have study space outside of their tanks—which are often noisy. Some of the inmates have asked about the GED program. At present, the public library is not providing GED study materials because its policy is not to provide multiple copies of textbooks or workbooks for class use.

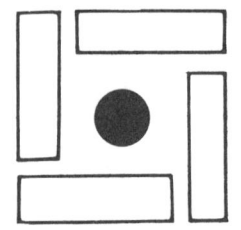

Case Study #2: The Ellis County Jail is a new facility housing 250 inmates. It was designed with an in-jail library in cooperation with the public library staff. It currently has a half-time librarian and two part-time library assistants. The jail provides adequate security for inmate visits twice a week for each tank. The library is well used by the inmates. Recently the teachers who work with the inmates have tried to include reentry information and materials in their curriculum. But they do not know how to locate information specific to their commuity. Also, many inmates who need reentry information do not attend adult education classes. The public library is currently cooperating with the local social services agency in updating a community services directory.

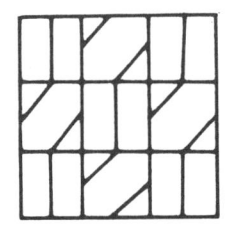

Conference on Improving Jail Library Service

Introduction

Setting and Length

This is a one- or two-day state or regional conference that can be held separately or as a preconference at a professional association meeting. It can be sponsored by a library and/or a correctional agency or an association, by a library school or a criminal justice institute, or an NIC area resource jail.

Number of Participants

Any number up to 100 to 125.

Target Audience

Participants do not need to be in a position to implement jail library service to attend. This type of conference is designed to provide up-to-date information on the topic for anyone interested in learning more about jail library service—librarians, jail staff, state agency consultants, library trustees and local government officials, and community agency staff.

Workshop Methods

This conference is based primarily on presentations by specialists in corrections and librarianship, combined with some small group discussion and a chance for participants to consult individually with specialists and other participants. *Jail Library Service* will be available at the conference for those who want to pursue initiating or expanding their own program of jail service. The conference design is based on the National Institute on Library Service to Jail Populations. For handouts and videotapes from the National Institute, write ASCLA, 50 East Huron St., Chicago, IL 60611.

Resource Persons

The workshop involves a number of resource persons, who give short presentations on specific content areas and are also available to consult individually with participants and serve as small group leaders.

1. The workshop coordinator who is a specialist in jail library service from the state or region, a resource person from the National Institute, or a state library institutional consultant
2. Public librarians and sheriffs who are involved in jail library service in different sizes of jails and with experience in different services—legal, education, reentry, staff services
3. Former inmates
4. Representatives from funding sources within the state or region—LSCA, LEAA, NEH, state library agency, state correctional

agency, local fund-raising efforts, libraries and jails who have received budget increases for jail library service
5. Correctional consultants knowledgeable in ACA and state jail standards, court decisions, security.

Workshop Goal

This conference will provide participants with up-to-date information on the status of jail library service in the state and region and nationally and will discuss different approaches to that service.

Workshop Objectives

Following the conference, library and correctional participants will be able to:

1. Identify the pros and cons of various service options for providing jail library service based on the needs within the facility and the resources available.
2. Cite people, organizations, or agencies they can contact for assistance in providing and expanding jail library service, including what they have learned about other participants' programs.
3. Identify services to assist the facility in meeting state and national standards.
4. Select a variety of formats of materials to better meet the needs and interests of inmates and jail staff, and discuss the pros and cons of each.
5. Identify various modes of delivery for jail services within the defined barriers and limitations of their facilities.
6. Identify techniques for assessing the library needs and interests of inmates and staff on a continuing basis.
7. Discuss techniques in solving or preventing internal problems created by lack of cooperation, interest, and understanding from librarians (for jail staff) or from jail staff (for librarians) or from inmates (for both).
8. Discuss methods of obtaining public support of the jail program.
9. Cite sources of funds on the local, state, and national levels that might be used to initiate or expand jail library service, and identify who they would contact about the availability of these funds.

Form Z Sample Agenda

Conference on Improving Jail Library Service
March 10-11, 198X

Agenda

March 10	8:00- 9:00 A.M.	Registration
	9:00- 9:30 A.M.	Introductions
	9:30-10:30 A.M.	The jail and the library
	10:30-10:45 A.M.	Break
	10:45-12 noon	Our patrons speak
	12:00- 1:00 P.M.	Lunch
	1:00- 3:00 P.M.	Looking at service programs--reentry, education, staff services, legal services
	3:00- 3:45 P.M.	View exhibits and consult with speakers
	3:45- 4:30 P.M.	What should the library do?
	7:00- 9:00 P.M.	Doing time
March 11	9:00-10:30 A.M.	Support for your program
	10:30-11:00 A.M.	View exhibits and consult with funding sources
	11:00-12 noon	Establishing jail library service
	12:00- 1:00 P.M.	Lunch
	1:00- 2:00 P.M.	The problems we face
	2:00- 2:45 P.M.	Jail library service: sheriff's view
	2:45- 3:00 P.M.	Evaluation

Workshop Coordinator: Barbara Mann, Institutional Consultant
State Library
Box 1234
Topeka, KS 66801

Sponsored by: State Library   State Sheriffs Association
Criminal Justice Institute

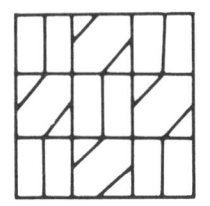

Conference Design

	First Day	
9–9:30	INTRODUCTIONS OF WORKSHOP COORDINATOR, PARTICIPANTS, AND AGENDA	30 minutes

9:30–10:30 THE JAIL AND THE LIBRARY 1 hour

Materials: Optional use of 16mm film or slides depicting jail library service (Appendix C) for part of presentation

Content: Jail librarian (or state library consultant) and sheriff (or other jail personnel) identify trends and issues for jail library service and jails.

1. State and national jail and library standards
2. Status of jail library service in state/region
3. Patterns of jail library service and descriptions of innovative library service.

10:30–10:45	BREAK	15 minutes

10:45–12 noon OUR PATRONS SPEAK 1 hour, 15 minutes

Content:

1. Present two or three short role plays between librarian and ex-offender that point out some of the problems with library service "inside."
   - *a)* The new librarian has trouble understanding inmates' street language and different culture. The librarian feels confused and somewhat intimidated.
   - *b)* An inmate desperately needs legal information for an upcoming court case and has a two-day deadline. The librarian promises to get this information, but is inundated with other work and does not follow up. The inmate is angry—and now has lost a chance for a rehearing of his case.
   - *c)* A naive librarian acts friendly and pleasant and does not realize that an inmate's interest in her is a "con" to get favors for special library privileges or to cover up his attempts to rip off library materials.
2. Ex-offender discusses needs for information and materials and services that the library seldom provides.
3. Jail staff member discusses staff needs for information and materials and services that the library seldom provides.

12–1	LUNCH	1 hour

1–3	LOOKING AT SERVICE PROGRAMS	2 hours

Materials: Jail Library Service, chapters 6–7, and displays

Content: Specialists each have 20 minutes to discuss the justification of the service, pros and cons, materials, and possible methods of providing the service: reentry, educational, legal, and staff services.

3–3:45	BREAK	45 minutes

Participants can view displays and talk to speakers individually or in small groups.

3:45–4:30	WHAT SHOULD THE LIBRARY DO?	45 minutes

Content: Small groups discuss possible role and services of the public library in the jail. Small groups are made up of jail and library staff and ex-inmates.

7–9	DOING TIME	2 hours

Options:
1. Social hour for informal sharing among participants and speakers
2. 16mm films and other nonprint materials (Appendix C)
3. "The Jail Library Game" (Appendix B)
4. Tour of local jail

SECOND DAY

9–10:30	SUPPORT FOR YOUR PROGRAM	1 hour, 30 minutes

Materials: Form I

Content: Workshop coordinator and knowledgeable corrections specialist discuss funds and consultant services available from different sources. Or you can invite representatives from each funding source to speak for 10 to 15 minutes.

10:30–11	BREAK	30 minutes

Participants can view exhibits and talk to representatives of funding sources individually.

11–12	HOW TO ESTABLISH JAIL LIBRARY SERVICE	1 hour

Materials: Jail Library Service, especially chapters 2–4

Content:
1. Jail librarian or workshop coordinator emphasizes planning steps and decisions.

2. Coordinator emphasizes importance of joint planning and decision making between librarians and jail administrators and staff.

12–1   LUNCH   1 hour

1–2   PROBLEMS WE FACE   1 hour
Materials: "Jail Library Game: Attitude Assessment" (Appendix B)

Content:

1. Small groups of jail and library staff choose three or four problems to brainstorm, or they can select items from the attitude assessment sheet (Appendix B).
2. Group members list ideas on newsprint and choose most likely solution.

2–2:45   JAIL LIBRARY SERVICE—   45 minutes
THE SHERIFF'S VIEW
Materials: Jail Library Service, chapter 1

Content:

1. Sheriff describes benefits of jail library service for the jail.
2. Sheriff indicates that library can help meet jail standards—not only for library service but also to help support other types of jail programs. (Cite examples from the *ACA Manual of Standards for Adult Local Detention Facilities.*)
3. Sheriff gives tips for overcoming problems in working with local sheriff and jail staff.

2:45–3   EVALUATION   15 minutes

APPENDIX A
Human Resources for Improving Jail Library Service

LIBRARIES

Association of Specialized and Cooperative Library Agencies (ASCLA)
50 East Huron Street, Chicago, Ill. 60611
(312) 944-6780

A division of the American Library Association, ASCLA includes state library agencies and institutional libraries. The American Correctional Association participates with ASCLA in the Joint Committee on Institution Libraries. The Library Service to Prisoners Section (LSPS) of ASCLA is the group most active in the area of jail library service. The Project on Library Service to Jail Populations (1979–80) was sponsored by ASCLA and was initiated by the LSPS Service to Local Jails Resolution Committee. As a result of this national jail project, ASCLA has the following materials and information available:

1. Resource file of persons and groups actively involved in jail library service
2. Copies of handouts and videotapes from the National Institute on Library Service to Jail Populations
3. File of information on any workshops held on jail library service
4. Names of participants and speakers from the National Institute.

Publications of interest available from ASCLA:

Survey of Library Service in Local Correctional Facilities. Compiled and edited by the Library Services to Prisoners Section. ASCLA, 1980. 270 pp. (ASCLA Survey)

"Summary of Cases Relating to Jail Library Services." Art Moen, Coordinating ed. Prepared for the National Institute on Library Service to Jail Populations, 1980. (preliminary edition)

American Library Association (ALA)
50 East Huron Street, Chicago, Ill. 60611
(312) 944-6780

Other divisions of ALA with relevant resources and information:

Public Library Association, especially the Alternative Education Programs Section
Office for Library Outreach Services
Social Responsibilities Round Table
Young Adult Services Division

STATE AND REGIONAL LIBRARY ASSOCIATIONS

Each state has a state library association, affiliated with ALA. There are also regional library associations made up of multistate areas. Most of these associations publish a periodical or newsletter. For a list of library associations, see:

ALA Handbook of Organization. American Library Association (annual)
Bowker Annual of Library and Book Trade Information. Bowker (annual)

State Libraries

Each state has a state library agency that administers state and federal (Library Services and Construction Act—LSCA) money for libraries and also has available consultant services. Most state library agencies have institutional or outreach consultants who would be particularly interested in jail library service. State library consultants can provide information on state jail standards, on public libraries that have jail service, and on library systems in the state. For a list of state library agencies and consultants, see:

> *American Library Directory.* Bowker (annual)
> *Directory of State Library Agencies, Special Consultants, and Related Organizations.* ASCLA (annual)

Public Libraries and Library Systems

For a list of public libraries and library systems in each state, contact your state library or see:

> *American Library Directory.* Bowker (annual)

For a list of public libraries serving jails, see:

> *Survey of Library Service in Local Correctional Facilities.* ASCLA, 1980. You will need to update this information by contacting your state library.

Library Schools

There are graduate library schools in many states and undergraduate library science programs in most states. Faculty and students would be interested in attending jail library workshops, might provide university facilities for hosting workshops, and might have faculty who could serve as resource people. For a list of library schools and undergraduate library science programs, see:

> *American Library Directory.* Bowker (annual)

Corrections

American Correctional Association (ACA)
4321 Hartwick Road, L-208, College Park, Md. 20740
(301) 864-1070

The largest professional association for the entire field of corrections, ACA has established and published standards for various aspects of the corrections system, including jails and juvenile detention facilities. Publications of interest:

> *National Jail and Adult Detention Directory.* ACA (annual) (Jail Directory)
> A comprehensive list of jails in the United States, their administrators, and programs; indicates which states have state jail inspection units.
> *Directory of Correctional Institutions and Agencies.* ACA (annual)

Describes each state department of corrections and its staffing patterns, as well as correctional service agencies, LEAA regional offices, and state planning agencies.

ACA Manual of Standards for Adult Local Detention Facilities. ACA, 1979.

This manual includes standards for jail library service, as well as standards for all types of service programs in jails. Currently being revised.

CONtact, Inc.
P.O. Box 81826, Lincoln, Nebr. 68501
(402) 464-0602

This is a nonprofit organization in the field of criminal justice and human services, providing consultation, speakers, information services, and a broad range of publications.

National Ex-Offender Assistance Directory
CONtact Newsletter (monthly)
Corrections Compendium
   Highlights and surveys a current topic each month
1979 Jail Survey. 4 volumes.

National Sheriffs Association (NSA)
1250 Connecticut Ave., Suite 320, Washington, D.C. 20036
(202) 872-0422

Publications include *National Sheriff* (bimonthly).

National Jail Association (NJA)
Address changes annually as presidents change.

NJA holds its annual conference with the American Correctional Association's Congress of Corrections and publishes a bimonthly newsletter and the *National Jail Forum* (quarterly).

National Jail Managers Association
Address changes annually as presidents change.
Publishes a monthly newsletter.

National Institute of Corrections (NIC) Jail Center
P.O. Box 9130, Boulder, Colo. 80301
(303) 443-7050

The NIC Jail Center can provide names and information about possible resource people in the jail field, and can sometimes provide free consultants and trainers for workshops. They have a National Information Center with information and materials about jails. Currently there are six area resource center jails: Boulder, Colorado; New Haven, Connecticut; Fort Scott, Kansas; New Orleans, Louisiana; Rockville, Maryland; and Corvallis, Oregon. Six additional area resource jails will be designated.

State Correctional Associations

Many states have state correctional associations, some of which are affiliated with ACA. There are also state sheriffs associations. Contact your state department of corrections for this information. Most of these state associations have newsletters or periodicals. Many sponsor training events, have annual conferences, and maintain a legislative liaison with appropriate committees of the state legislature.

CRIMINAL JUSTICE INSTITUTES

Many major state universities have criminal justice departments or schools. Many of these offer training and continuing education programs for corrections personnel, as well as courses for university students at the undergraduate and graduate levels. Many criminal justice institutes provide training for sheriffs and other jail personnel and publish a calendar of training opportunities. Some criminal justice institutes have their own training facilities. Contact your state department of corrections for information on your state.

STATE DEPARTMENTS OF CORRECTIONS

Each state has a department of corrections to administer its prison system. In some states they will also administer juvenile facilities or local or regional jails. Some states have mandatory training programs for corrections personnel. For information on state departments of corrections in each state, see:

Directory of Correctional Institutions and Agencies. ACA (annual)

BOARDS OR COMMISSIONS ON CORRECTIONS

Each state has an official body to set standards for jail operations, grant variances, inspect jails, and work with the Office of Criminal Justice Planning. These boards or commissions may be a part of a department of corrections, the attorney general's office, a department of social welfare, or be independent. Members of the board and board staff can serve as resource persons or workshop faculty. The board itself and its publications provide a means of publicizing jail library service or a workshop.

OFFICES OF CRIMINAL JUSTICE PLANNING

These agencies work closely with local police and correctional administrators and planners. They are the agencies that administer Law Enforcement Assistance Administration (LEAA) funds, and in some states they may be a possible source of funds for jail library training. They also would be a source of trainers. These agencies are listed in:

Directory of Correctional Institutions and Agencies. ACA (annual)

STATE JAIL INSPECTION SERVICES

Some states have jail inspection teams. Some of these agencies can provide technical assistance and training for local jails. For a list, see:

National Jail and Adult Detention Directory. ACA (annual)

Directory of State Jail Inspection Programs. National Sheriffs Association, 1978.

STATE PUBLIC DEFENDERS

Public defenders have taken the lead in providing legal reference materials to jail inmates. They might be an excellent source of workshop faculty or instructional materials. For a list, see:

Directory of State Administrative Officials. Lexington, Kentucky: Council of State Governments.

LOCAL JAILS

For a list of local jails, their programs and administrators, see:

National Jail and Adult Detention Directory. ACA (annual) (Jail Directory)

EX-OFFENDERS

American Association of Ex-Offenders in Criminal Justice
c/o American Correctional Association
4321 Hartwick Road, L–208, College Park, Md. 20740
(301) 846-1070

CONtact, Inc.
P.O. Box 81826, Lincoln, Nebr. 68501
(402) 464-0602

National Ex-Offender Assistance Directory
Although primarily a listing of agencies and associations providing services to ex-offenders, these would be good contacts for locating ex-offenders willing to participate in jail library workshops, as well as social agency staff who might also be willing to be speakers.

Fortune Society
229 Park Avenue South, New York, N.Y. 10003
(212) 677-4600

This national association assists ex-offenders and helps identify ex-offenders who are willing to speak to different groups. It publishes a monthly newsletter.

Offender Aid and Restoration, U.S.A. (OAR)
409 East High Street, Charlottesville, Va. 22901
(804) 295-6196

OAR trains volunteers (including ex-inmates) to work with jail inmates while they are in jail and after release. It currently operates twenty-two programs in eight states with plans to expand. Publications include *OAR News* (quarterly) and a jail simulation ($110).

THE JAIL LIBRARY GAME

START

Attitude Reflection
What is Jail Library Service Really like?

Will my Director support me?

FINISH!
It can be done

HRLSD-LIBRARY SERVICE
TO PRISONERS SECTION
has designed a game simulation
for public service oriented librarians who
are interested in establishing a jail library program.
The players will proceed from table to table where they
will be challenged to match wits with a sheriff, library
administrator, people responsible for funding and pressure groups such as inmates and teachers.
Come if you want some practical experience in establishing jail
libraries or just fun.

Come Saturday, June 24, 1978

Time: 2 p.m.-4 p.m.

Place: Palmer House--Parlor F

Sponsors: Association of Specialized and Cooperative
Library Agencies--Library Service to Prisoners
Section and Public Library Association

Funding

LSCA

Donations

Public Libraries

LEAA

Religious Groups

visit jail

Meet the Sheriff

$ $ $ $

APPENDIX B
The Jail Library Game

Designed by Conference Program Committee, 1978
Library Service to Prisoners Section
Association of Specialized and Cooperative Library Agencies,
a division of the American Library Association, Chicago, Illinois

The Jail Library Game was designed by a team of institutional librarians for a program presented at the 1978 American Library Association's Annual Conference. The program, sponsored by the Health and Rehabilitative Library Services Division's* Library Service to Prisoners Section, was implemented by 35 HRLSD members, and a total of 58 people participated in the game.

The game attempts to acquaint persons interested in library services to jails by simulating some of the steps that need to be accomplished before library service to a jail can be established. Utilizing this overview and the guide sheets for the game, a group with some experience in the area of jail library service should be able to replicate the game. The guide sheets also will help any librarian, library administrator, or sheriff contemplating or initiating jail library service.

PLANNING THE GAME
1. Review the guide sheets to gain a sense of what needs to be accomplished at each station.
2. Locate people who can fulfill the necessary roles needed to staff the game (see fig. 1).
3. Consider the suggested floor plan to gain a sense of the physical requirements for the jail library game (see fig. 2).
4. Consider the size of the room available to your group and design the floor plan for easy flow of traffic.
5. Decide what the maximum time limit should be at each station. At ALA, it was 10 minutes. You may wish to use a longer period of time.
6. Decide whether or not people can join the game at any time or whether all participants need to be starting together. At ALA, persons were allowed to start any time during the first two hours of the 2½ hour program slot. Participants usually completed the game in an hour.
7. Acquaint all staffers with their role before the presentation of the game. We found that this could be done by mail and phone calls prior to the conference.
8. Have a meeting the day of presenting the game so that the staffers understand how they all function within the context of the game. If time is available, the planning committee should conduct a run through of the game so that the staffers become familiar with the logistics.

THE PARTICIPANTS
Participants will enter the room, be asked to sign in and be seated. Either as people arrive or once all participants have arrived, the guard will give instructions on how the game is played and hand out the attitude assessment. The attitude assessment is to be used privately by the participant as a means to evoke some of the emotions and present some of the problems and situations that arise in providing jail library service. The participant can just think, jot down quick answers, or respond however he or she feels appropriate. When the guard senses that the participant has responded to the attitude assessment in some manner and is ready to move on, the guard will either assign or direct the participant to one of the stations (library administrators, sheriffs, funding consultants).

*HRLSD is now part of the Association of Specialized and Cooperative Library Agencies (ASCLA).

Appendix B

Position	Responsibilities	Characteristics
Guard(s)	Sign people in. Hand out attitude assessment. Introduce game (stations, where to go if confused, role play). Be able to direct people through game.	Dress in uniform (if possible). Able to respond to people's feelings surfaced by the attitude assessment.
Library Administrator(s)	Role play with participants to bring out the items that need to be considered by a public library administrator and the library's governing body. Provide an individual growth experience by presenting various positions to each participant. For example, if the participant is self-assured, ask difficult questions and be hesitant about providing jail library service and if the participant is uncertain, be supportive in the discussion and surface the questions with which the participant should be dealing.	Able to role play the part as well as participate in a discussion on the topic for those who are uncomfortable with role playing. Knowledge of the various positions which library administrators have taken on this type of service and why.
Sheriff(s)	Role play with participants to make them aware of the problems (i.e., security, drain on staff time, cost) that jail library service can bring up. Discuss the possible alternatives to these problems. Help participants to realize that they need to be solid in their presentation to sheriffs in the future. To provide an individual growth experience by presenting various positions to each participant. For example, if the participant is self-assured, ask difficult questions and be hesitant about providing jail library service and if the participant is uncertain, be supportive in the discussion and surface the questions with which the participant should be dealing.	Able to role play the part as well as participate in a discussion on the topic for those who are uncomfortable with role playing. Background as a guard or jail administrator is helpful. Knowledge of a jail with library service.

Funding Consultant(s)	Role play with participants to help them brainstorm on how to build a library service program with little or no financial support.	Able to role play the part as well as participate in a discussion on the topic for those who are uncomfortable with role playing. Knowledge of freebies, tapping local funding sources, grants.
Pressure Group(s)	To stimulate, through questions, the various types of requests which will be made of a librarian in a jail. May approach any number of participants. Represents pressure groups in a jail such as educators, guards, inmates, religious groups.	Able to easily approach people as there is no planned time for this part of the game; the pressurer just "confronts" the person between stations. Previous thinking about the questions so that they can feel comfortable discussing the problem which the question poses.
Floating Consultant(s)	To help guide people from station to station. To answer participants' questions. To conduct evaluation if desired.	Complete understanding of the logistics of the game. Good background in jail library service in order to field all questions.

Figure 1. Descriptions of Staffers

At each station, the participant and staffer should spend a set amount of time dealing with the topic. The staffer will utilize the appropriate guide sheet as a basis for catalyzing a discussion with the participant on the identified topic. Once the discussion is completed or the designated time period at the station has passed, the staffer should give a copy of the guide sheet to the participant for future reference. The participant is then ready to go to another station. Rather than have participants go through the game in a set sequence, it is better to direct them to a station where there is a staffer available.

While moving or waiting between stations, the participants should be confronted by at least one pressure group representative.

There are several ways to determine when a participant has completed the game. Staff can ask the participant, check that the participant has all the guide sheets, or draw up a check sheet that can be marked at each station. At the ALA meeting, the guards and consultants just asked. Once the participant has visited all stations, a floating consultant should approach them to see if they have any unanswered questions, show them the resource table, and conduct an evaluation, if desired.

HELPFUL HINTS
1. All staffers need to be knowledgeable about their topic, sensitive to people, and flexible in how they interact with each participant.
2. The jail library game could be expanded to include a legal materials component.
3. Decide ahead on the length of the program, the number of people who can participate, the number of staffers needed/available, the time an individual can spend on the attitude assessment, and the time spent with each consultant.
4. Signs should be made to identify all stations and persons' roles involved in the game.

RESOURCE LIST

American Correctional Association. *Providing Legal Services for Prisoners: A Tool for Correctional Administrators.* College Park, Md.: ACA, 1977. 53p. $4.00

American Correctional Association Committee on Institution Libraries. *Library Standards for Adult Correctional Institutions. Draft II.* Louisville, Ky.: ACA, 1975.

Association of Hospital and Institution Libraries Special Committee on Library Service to Prisoners. *Jails Need Libraries, Too!* Chicago: American Library Association, 1974. 16p. $.75

Commission on Accreditation for Corrections. *Manual of Standards for Adult Local Detention Facilities.* Rockville, Md.: Commission on Accreditation for Corrections, 1977.

Illinois Libraries 56: 501–82 (Sept. 1974).

Illinois State Library Ad Hoc Committee on County Jail Library Standards. *Library Recommendations for County Jail Standards Made to the Illinois Department of Corrections.* Springfield, Ill.: Illinois State Library, 1974.

LeDonne, Marjorie. "Summary of Court Decisions Relating to the Provision of Library Services in Correctional Institutions." In *Bowker Annual of Library and Book Trade Information.* New York: Bowker, 1974, p. 91–102. Available also in pamphlet form from ALA, $1.00.

Library Trends 26: 301–446 (Winter 1978).

Wilson Library Bulletin 51: 496–553 (Feb. 1977).

Also:
   Books available on the prison experience
   Locally produced prison newsletters
   Grant proposals (LSCA, LEAA)

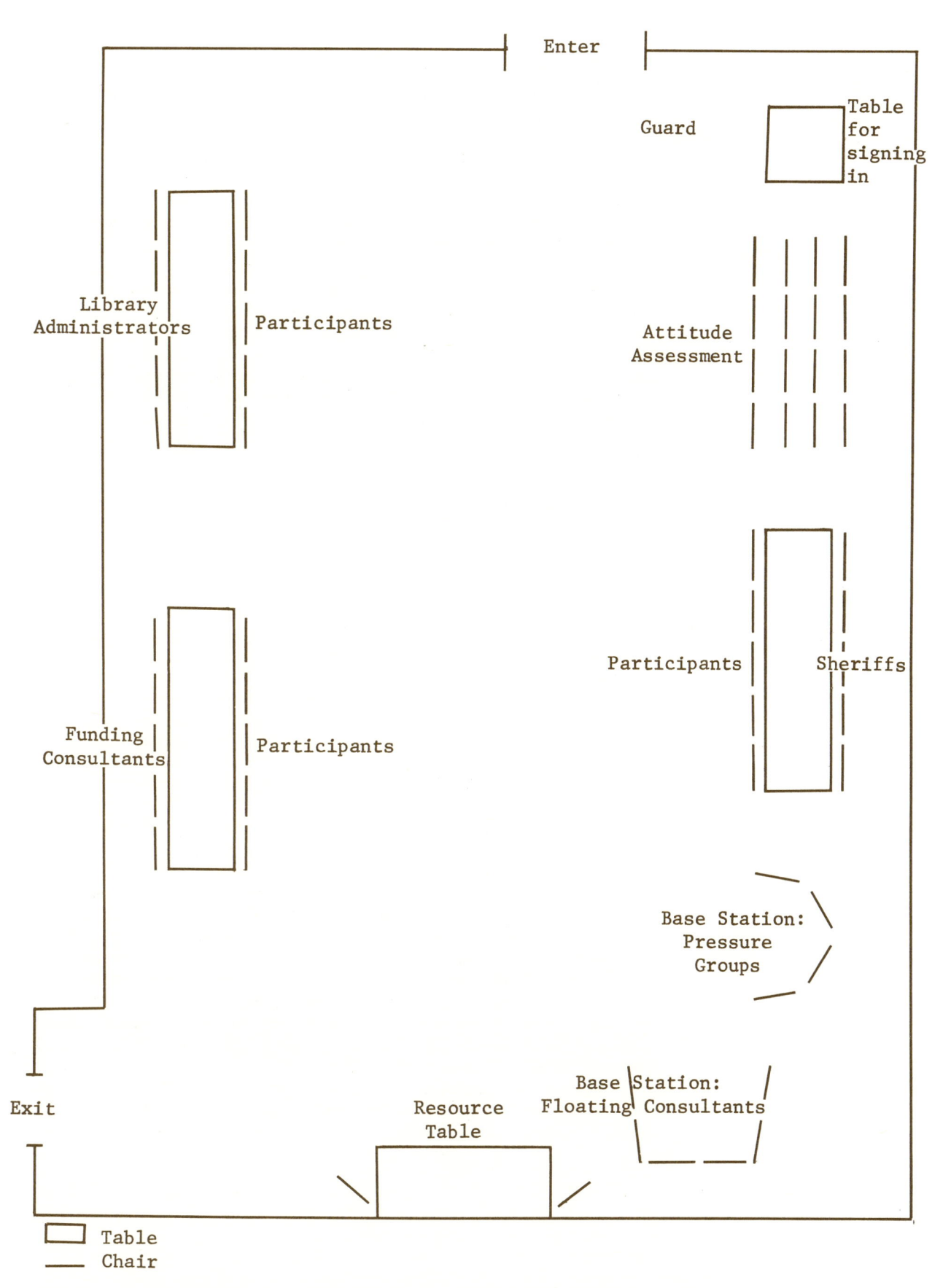

Figure 2. A Suggested Floor Plan for the Jail Library Game

ATTITUDE ASSESSMENT

Read This First! It is important for you to understand that this questionnaire is for you to examine some of your own attitudes toward this specialized library service. There are no correct answers; you will not be graded or judged; in fact, you are the only one who needs to see this sheet. Please take the time to read each question carefully and think about your answers. Writing something down will give you a better opportunity at the end of the day (or in six months) to evaluate your feelings. After this program, we encourage you to talk with others about any questions which you find disturbing.

1. Have you ever done anything for which, if you had been observed, you could have been arrested?
2. Although the selection policy agreed upon by the sheriff states that only a limited range of materials will be excluded from the jail, the guard at the door refuses to let you bring in the Harold Robbins books because of the sex scenes. How do you handle this? What type of books can you justify excluding from the jail?
3. Some people assume that most inmates are black and dumb. What do you think?
4. You are permitted to visit the isolation cells once a month. Although the inmates in isolation may have only one book, an inmate asks you for more because he's afraid he'll go insane if he doesn't have something to keep him busy. How do you approach the authorities to modify the rules?
5. Are donated "attic collections," such as 20 years of *Reader's Digest,* better than no books at all?
6. Four heavy metal doors have locked behind you. You will now spend the next 3 hours with inmates, guards, and books. You do not have access to a telephone or a window or privacy and will constantly hear the sounds of the jail. How do you feel?
7. If there is any harassment, is it likely to come from inmates or staff?
8. Throughout the day you are interrupted with questions that seem simplistic and unnecessary because some inmates see you more as a contact to the outside than as a librarian. Does this role aggravate you? How do you handle the situation when inmates need to talk rather than read?
9. Who is "us"? Who is "them"? Is "us/them" necessary?
10. You are walking down a corridor with cells on either side and a loud and luring whistle is made. What do you do? You are suddenly aware that an inmate is making a play for you. How do you handle this?
11. (a) Inmates ask for law books. When you try to find out what they need, the sergeant tells you that his men are there to answer legal questions and to supply law books and for you to stay out of it. Knowing that the books are not supplied, what do you do? (b) The sheriff has asked for your patrons' reading records. What do you do? (c) What are prisoners' legal rights?
12. Do you see yourself as a rescuer? Is punishment rehabilitative?
13. Several hostage situations have been reported by the media recently. Does your fear of being taken hostage affect your job performance, or the type of services you offer, or the way you treat inmates?
14. You've been told by inmates that the guards are creaming off the best books for themselves. Considering the implications, how do you handle this?
15. Requests for books on psychology, poetry, and Egyptian art surprise you. Why?

16. How do you feel about knowing, or not knowing, whether the person you are talking with is doing time for shoplifting, murder, or rape?
17. How do you handle the following requests? Any Donald Goines book? A $45 art book? Law books? Crossword puzzles? *Playboy? Playgirl?* Interlibrary loan material?
18. The sheriff has just told you that you cannot have paperbacks in the jail because they will be stuffed into the toilets. The sheriff has just told you that you cannot have hardbacks in the jail because they can be used as weapons. What do you do?
19. The jail library subscribes to ten copies of *Jet*, yet there are still more needed to meet the demand. Will you try to justify this?
20. On your rounds, you observe a guard shouting and kicking at an inmate who is being forced to clean the toilets with his or her own shirt. How do you handle reporting this? As you round a corner, you encounter two inmates embracing and kissing. How do you handle reporting this?
21. After six months of working in the jail library, you suddenly realize that you have never enjoyed a job as much. Why is this so?
22. Even though you think your collection of best sellers will be a hit, you find that the books don't circulate. How do you find out the reading interests and information needs of your inmate population?
23. Several guards, who have access to outside libraries, have asked you if they can use the jail library. Considering the inmates' limited access to libraries versus the staff relations aspect, what will your policy be on staff usage?
24. You've been asked by an inmate to make a phone call to his family once you are on the outside again. What do you do?
25. There are some sensational aspects of jail library service. What is your responsibility to coworkers, inmates, and your own friends to explain your job?
26. An inmate has little, if any, private space or time. Can you imagine yourself in this situation for a year?
27. Each time you enter the jail, the rules seem to change a bit. Sometimes you are searched; other times you are not. Sometimes you are treated with respect; other times you are treated as a real intruder. Once, your vitamin capsules were suspected as contraband. How do you feel about these fluctuations?
28. You have spent an inordinate amount of time in the past few months training inmate assistants who are then transferred or released. Is it important to keep on doing this?
29. Deputies are supposed to be in a support role; how do you feel when they make passes at you?
30. How do you feel about guards having periodical shakedowns to retrieve overdue or stolen materials?
31. Think about handing books through bars to people on the other side.
32. How do you feel when you see a person weaken physically and mentally week by week?
33. An inmate tells you that you and the library are the only things that keep him sane while he is locked up. How do you feel?

QUESTIONS FOR THE SHERIFFS TO ASK

Should a library be established?
1. What would you be doing in the jail?
2. Do you realize that there are some very tricky politics involved in working with both inmates and staff?
3. We get donated books and their relatives send them books. How many books do you feel they need?
4. If you are injured in the course of your work here, who is liable?
5. Would it bother you to be shaken down every time you come into the jail?
6. Don't you feel that it would be too dangerous to have women work in the back section of the jail?

How valuable would the library service be?
1. Do you know that books can be used to smuggle in contraband?
2. Do you feel that guards should be used to bring inmates to the library when they could be used for more essential duties elsewhere?
3. We don't even have room for an indoor exercise area. Is a library more important?
4. Books can be a fire hazard, they can be used as weapons, and they can be used to plug up the plumbing. How can you make sure they are used for the right purposes?

How will the library be run?
1. How would censorship be decided?
2. Can offensive books be seized?
3. Wouldn't more lawsuits against us result from your bringing in law books?
4. Would you be willing to perform the work of the guards if we needed you?

ADMINISTRATOR'S CHECKLIST

Instructions: Ask participant which 2 or 3 areas (roman numerals) are most likely to deal with their anticipated problems. Then discuss those. Participants get a copy of the complete checklist to take home.

I. Budget
1. How much will service to prisoners cost the library?
2. Are there other sources of funding than the library budget?
3. Who would be responsible for writing grant applications?
4. What is the legal status of library service to prisoners in our state? Are there standards we would have to observe?
5. Basic line items to estimate for budgeting service: personnel, materials, supplies, equipment, printing and duplication, transportation.
6. Would bookmobile service be a less costly solution?

II. Staffing
1. Who can do it? Can we use someone part-time who is already on staff?
    a) Will the sheriff allow a woman to come into the jail?
    b) Will they do some checking into the person's background?
    c) What personality traits would be helpful for that job?
2. Is more than one person needed, with different skills? How much clerical work is involved?
3. How about training a substitute for emergencies?
4. How much time per week is needed to serve the average population of the jail?
5. What kind of schedule are we talking about? Do the jailers pretty much define when library service can take place?
6. Where will this staff be working—in the library or in jail, or both?

III. Materials Selection
1. How much and what kind of materials will we need?
    a) How will we provide legal reference information/popular law books?
    b) Are there prisoners in need of foreign language materials? Large print materials?
    c) Are we going to use paperbacks, hardcover books, or a mixture?
    d) Does the sheriff place any restrictions on format or content?
    e) What if these restrictions conflict with our library policies? Is there any authority to appeal to?
    f) Should we purchase new materials for the jail library, or use books already in the collection, or withdrawn books, or donations—or a combination, maybe?
2. Will there be damage and destruction of materials?
3. What special retrieval methods might we have to use to assure some degree of circulation control? This would affect our inventory of popular titles.
4. How would we handle special requests for a certain title, author, or subject? Purchase? Check out from main library? Reserve? Interlibrary loan?

IV. Technical Processing
1. Is it worthwhile doing full cataloging and classification for jail?
2. How much processing is absolutely necessary?
    a) Will you need a title file? A shelflist?
    b) Will books need cards and pockets for the checkout procedure you are planning?
    c) Is reinforcement of paperback and magazine spines a good idea?
3. Who should process the books—regular technical processing staff or jail library staff?
4. What about mending books to increase their circulation "mileage"?
5. Is speed a factor in processing for prisoners?
6. How will the processed materials be transported from library to jail?

V. Procedures
1. How will you handle checking materials out and in?
2. Can you promise reasonably reliable statistics, both totals and breakdowns?
3. How will you develop cooperation of other library staff members on this venture, when you may be risking "their" books?
4. How can we keep track of requests? Forms?
5. Would an institutional checkout card for the jail library be the best way to handle filling requests from the main library collection? What about a dummy checkout card for prisoners to sign?

QUESTIONS FROM PRESSURE GROUPS

1. We are implementing a crash GED program in our jail. Can you supply the practice manual for all 50 residents? (Teacher)
2. The brothers want their special edition of the Koran. Can you get one copy for each of them? (Inmate)
3. Can I take this law book back to my cell? (Inmate)
4. Can you do the research and write a writ for me? (Inmate)
5. We would like for you to buy the last ten years of the *Chilton's Manual* for the manual training class which is forming. (Teacher)
6. Please put Chaplain Ray's ministry materials in the library. (Chaplain)
7. Since the visiting gallery is so crowded on Sundays, would you let us use the library for additional visiting space? (Security)
8. We have ten inmates waiting to meet the Board of Pardons and Paroles. Can they wait in the library? (Security)
9. Can you get a copy of *Icebird Slim* for us? (Inmate)
10. There is a chemical called manganese dioxide. What are its properties and what does it do? (Inmate)
11. Can I work in the library? (A known troublemaker among the inmates)

SOURCES OF FUNDING AND MATERIALS

I. Libraries (Public, academic, special, government)
1. Have you considered support from the library?
2. To what extent will support be given? What kind of support can be expected?
   Staffing at jail?
   Bookmobile service?
   Funds for books and materials?
   Technical processing?
3. Have you considered support from the Friends of the Library?
4. What other kinds of library support could be developed?
   Phone reference
   Trustee funds
   Xerox

II. Grants
1. Have you considered obtaining a grant?
2. To what extent will support be given to you in applying for a grant?
   Do you have the skills to write a proposal?
   Are there workshops in your area dealing with grantsmanship that you can attend?
3. Have you considered grants from:
   CETA
   LSCA (probably through the state library)
   Law Enforcement Assistance Administration
   Private foundations (check the *Foundations Directory*)
   Revenue Sharing

III. Institutions
1. Have you considered support from the institution?
2. To what extent will support be given for:
   Staffing?
   Space?
   Funds for books and materials?
   Line items in budget?
3. Have you considered support from:
   Sheriff's budget
   Residents' welfare fund
   Resident organizations

IV. Donations
1. Have you considered obtaining donations, either monetary of books?
2. How would you go about obtaining donations?
3. If there are book donations, would you try to control the quality and if so, how?
4. Have you considered support from:
   Rotary
   American Society of Friends
   American Association of University Women
   Community service groups
   Legal associations
   Lions
   League of Women Voters
   Church groups
   Other local organizations

V. Free Materials
1. Have you considered obtaining free materials?
2. How would you go about locating them?
3. Have you considered support from:
   Post office
   Book stores
   Radio stations
   Magazine distributors or publishers
   Bibliographies listing sources of free materials

APPENDIX C
Jail and Prison Films and Other Nonprint Materials

This list is a compilation, by no means complete, of 16mm films and other nonprint materials produced after 1960 on jail and prison life. No attempt has been made to verify that the films and other materials are still available from distributors because many of the items are available through rental collections or lending libraries.

The following resources were used in compiling this list:
Boston Public Library film catalog
Boston University Film Library catalog, 1978–1980
Corrections Compendium
Educational Film Locator, 1978
"Frame-Up: The Prison Experience on Film," a bibliography compiled by Diane Davenport and the SRRT Task Force on Service to Prisoners
Index to 16mm Educational Films
Inside-Outside
New England Invitational Prison Art Show flyer
Positive Images: Non-Sexist Films for Young People by Susan Wengraf and Linda Aetel
Wilson Library Bulletin, April and May 1977.

A la Brava: Prison and Beyond. 54 min., b&w, 1975. Extension Service Media Center, University of California, Berkeley, Calif. 94720.
Filmed details of daily life in California's Soledad Prison; motivations, ambitions, and intellectual insights of Chicano inmates.

Alcatraz, Parts 1 & 2. 56 min., color, 1977. TMS Films Limited, 2209 N. Central Ave., Glendale, Calif. 91203.
Presents information available in the 1970s, including interviews and newsreel footage, in order to unravel the mysteries about Alcatraz prison.

And the Walls Came Tumbling Down. 26 min., b&w, 1975. Extension Service Media Center, University of California, Berkeley, Calif. 94720.
An intense documentary of an improvisational drama workshop conducted by Martha Kimbrell with inmates of the Queens House of Detention for Men in New York City.

Attica. 90 min., color, 1973. Tri-Continental Film Center West, P.O. Box 4430, Berkeley, Calif. 94704.
Documentary of the rebellion by prisoners at the state prison in Attica, New York.

Being a Prisoner. 28 min., color, 1975. Kinok, 137 E. 26th St., #1B, New York, N.Y. 10010.
This film makes a good case for the hypothesis that the inmates' lack of money for a good lawyer, rather than their danger to society, was the cause of incarceration. Prominence is given to the effects of separating mothers and children.

Born Innocent. 99 min., color, 1976. Learning Corporation of America, 1350 Avenue of the Americas, New York, N.Y. 10019.
The film presents a 13-year-old runaway girl whose parents make her a ward of the state and depicts the ensuing loss of the girl's innocence in a detention home where she lives with drug users and prostitutes.

Busted. 17 min., color, 1972. Paramount Communications, 5451 Marathon St., Hollywood, Calif. 90038.
Aimed directly at young people who have not yet decided what road to take,

---

Compiled by Marnie Warner, consultant on Library Services to the Disadvantaged, Massachusetts Board of Library Commissioners; assisted by Delores Stapp, School of Library Science, Emporia State University, Emporia, Kansas.

the film shows what it is like to be tried in juvenile court and to be put in juvenile hall.

Cages. 9 min., 1963. Contemporary/McGraw-Hill Films, Distribution Center, Princeton Road, Hightstown, N.J. 08520.

In this animated film a warden brings a prisoner toy blocks but takes them away when the prisoner proves that he is too skillful with them.

Canada behind Bars. 25 min., color, 1976. CTV Television Network, 48 Charles St. E, Toronto, Ontario Canada.

A correspondent reports on Canada's prison population, which in proportion to population is among the highest in number in the world.

The Caring Community Corrects: A Reflection on Community Involvement. Slide/tape. Modern Media Office, Archdiocese of Kansas City, 2220 Central Ave., Kansas City, Kans. 66102.

Focuses on increasing society's awareness of its responsibility to correct the offender rather than punish. Presents examples of community-based corrections programs in operation in several states and notes that the primary core of these alternatives is the involvement of people in caring communities.

Case for Reform. 30 min., color, 1970. WCAU-TV, City Line E Monument Ave., Philadelphia, Pa. 19131.

Pictures a reporter as he visits Bucks County Prison in Pennsylvania and talks with the warden, prisoners, and nearby residents about the prison rehabilitative projects, which include private visitation, community jobs with pay, free bail, and a grievance council.

Cell 16. 14 min., color, 1971. National Film Board of Canada, 680 Fifth Ave., Suite 819, New York, N.Y. 10019.

Shows the effects of confinement on the person in prison.

Children in Trouble: Alternatives to a National Scandal. 29 min., color, 1974. The Film Makers Inc., 290 West Avenue, New York, N.Y. 10023.

This visually strong film allows kids in jail to speak for themselves as it examines the existing scandalous situation in juvenile "rehabilitation centers" and proposes practical and effective alternatives to the system.

The Cloister. 19 min., b&w, silent. Filmakers' Cooperative, 175 Lexington Ave., New York, N.Y. 10016.

A film by Gretchen Langheld, from a screenplay by Andrea Sworkin. "A woman's experience at the NYC House of Detention for Women."

Crime's Forgotten Children. 27 min., color, 1976. Modern Talking Picture Service, 2323 New Hyde Road, New Hyde Park, N.Y. 11040.

Presents the story of the Bethel Bible School, the only U.S. home exclusively for the children of prison inmates.

Criminal Justice in the U.S. 32 min., b&w, 1966. Films Incorporated, 1144 Wilmette Ave., Wilmette, Ill. 60091.

Unique study of the gap between the ideals and the realities of criminal justice. Reviews the cases of twelve convicted men, each of whom was later proved innocent.

Crowded—The Baltimore City Jail. 15 min., color, 1977. Cinema Leap.

Documents the overcrowded conditions of the city jail in Baltimore. Draws attention to the psychological and moral oppression of the American penal system.

Cutting Up Old Touches. 30 min., color, 1976. Odeon, Box 315, Franklin Lakes, N.J. 07417.

Biography of a person who has spent most of his life in a series of prisons.

Dark Corner of Justice. 39 min., color, 1970. National Broadcasting Co., 30 Rockefeller Plaza, New York, N.Y. 10020.

Documents the conditions suffered by prisoners awaiting trial in the Cuyahoga County Jail in Ohio.

Dark Corner of Justice. 58 min., color, 1970. WKYC-TV, 1403 E. 6th St., Cleveland, Ohio 44114.

Points out the conditions in Cleveland jails that have made individuals accused of crimes a forgotten segment of society.

Dead Man Coming. 24 min., b&w, 1973. Pyramid, Box 1048, Santa Monica, Calif. 90406.

Contrasts opinions of the rehabilitation programs. While former convicts explain how unprepared for the outside a person is when freed, the warden says that rehabilitation programs draw criticism from people who think prisons are too lenient.

Death Row. 49 min., color, 1972. Time-Life Films, 43 W. 16th St., New York, N.Y. 10011.

On June 28, 1972, the Supreme Court made its historic decision abolishing the death penalty in America. This film, made shortly before that decision, puts the complex legal, social, and moral issues into perspective.

Emotional Disturbances in a Correctional Facility. 16 min., color, 1976. AIMS Instructional Media Services, Inc., 626 Justin Avenue, Glendale, Calif. 91201.

Discusses human frailties, such as lying, forgetting, and preoccupation. Analyzes signs which indicate that these frailties are growing into real emotional disturbances among the inmates.

Escape. 27 min., color, 1975. McMaster University, Hamilton, Ont., Canada.

Portrays a new prisoner discovering the loneliness of a prison cell.

Four Gray Walls. 29 min., color, 1973. Brigham Young University, Green House, Provo, Utah 84602.

Of the 160 convicts who participated in the Family Home Evening Program and were released from prison over a four-year period only two returned. This recidivism rate is less than 2 percent compared to a national rate of 80 percent.

Gerst. 15 min., color, 1976. Robert A. Ferretti.

Deals with a character whose fantasies and self-delusions are stripped away slowly in the hard reality of a prison environment.

The Glass House. 90 min., color, 1972. Learning Corporation of America, 1350 Avenue of the Americas, New York, N.Y. 10019.

A movie for television by Truman Capote, filmed in the Utah State Prison. This story is a gripping cry for prison reform.

Holidays . . . Hollow Days. 59 min., b&w, 1973. Indiana University Audiovisual Center, Bloomington, Ind. 47401.

This film touches on the dependency syndrome and the ineffectiveness of rehabilitation.

How Two Libraries Take Books behind Bars. 10 min., sound-slide program, 1978. Available from Darien Fisher, Special Services Librarian, State Library Commission of Iowa, Historical Building, Des Moines, Iowa 50319. (515) 281–4102.

Produced by the Iowa City Public Library and the Des Moines Public Library to detail how they provide jail library service.

I Am My Brother's Keeper. 40 min., color, sound, 1978. Distributed by Harper & Row Media.

A filmed documentary of a project at Rahway State Prison, New Jersey, designed to keep juvenile delinquents out of prison by showing them a realistic view of the harsh and cruel prison life.

I Live in Prison. 26 min., color, 1976. Learning Corporation of America, 1350 Avenue of Americas, New York, N.Y. 10019.

The California Institution for Men in Chino, California, allows a volunteer group of convicts to talk regularly to community groups about their lives as criminals. The convict group is called Prison Preventers. Their goal is to help others avoid prison by avoiding crime.

I'd Rather Be a Blind Man. 60 min., color, 1972. Extension Media Center, University of California, 2223 Fulton St., Berkeley, Calif. 94720.

Presents a cinema-vérité study of the daily routine of seven parole agents. Features parolees speaking about prison and their life outside.

I'm Gonna Be Free. 28 min., color, 1972. Paulist Communications, 17575 Pacific Coast Highway, P.O. Box 1057, Pacific Palisades, Calif. 90272.

A 15-year veteran of the prison system, Mylo makes his yearly appearance before the parole board. His impassioned bid for freedom exposes the underside of prison life. Based on a true story.

Insiders (Prison Life). 22 min., color, 1970. National Broadcasting Co., 30 Rockefeller Plaza, New York, N.Y. 10020.

Filmed by a convict filmmaker at the Missouri State Penitentiary, *Insiders* shows life at the penitentiary through the inmates' eyes.

Jail. 25 min., color, 1979. Distributed by Artvision, 140 E. 81st St., New York, N.Y. 10028.

A straight message from young people already in jail to young people who think they won't ever be in jail. Gets the message across without using scare tactics or rough language.

Jail Simulation Guide. $110 for complete plans for conducting the simulation. For further information: Offender Aid and Restoration, U.S.A., 409 E. High St., Charlottesville, Va. 22901. (804) 295-6196.

Jane Kennedy—To Be Free. 27 min., color, 1973. Indiana University, Bloomington, Ind. 47401.

A young Chicago nurse, who had been working within the political system, becomes involved in the civil rights and antiwar movements, to the point of being imprisoned. Her experiences with the prison system and the administration of individual justice are brought forth in her dialogue.

Joe Summerville. 26 min., color, 1975. Mississippi Authority for Educational Television, 3825 Ridgewood Road, Jackson, Miss. 39205.

Joe Summerville, a black inmate at Mississippi State Penitentiary and winner of the Southern AAU Boxing Championships, discusses his past and future.

Justice? 59 min., b&w, 1971. Indiana University, Bloomington, Ind. 47401.

Examines racism in United States courts and prisons, focusing on the cases of Angela Davis and the Soledad Brothers.

Juvenile Court. 144 min., b&w. Zipporah Films, Inc., 54 Lewis Wharf, Boston, Mass. 02110.

An unnarrated documentary of a Memphis, Tennessee, juvenile court that processes 17,000 complaints each year, including drug addiction, armed robbery, prostitution, child molesting, child neglect, child beating, and incest.

Killing Time. 60 min., color, 1980. Kauffmann & Boyce Productions, P.O. Box 283, Allston, Mass. 02134.

A study of the Massachusetts step system. The film follows inmates from a maximum security institution at Walpole to medium security at Norfolk to minimum security at Framingham to a pre-release center in Boston.

Lansing Prison, a Penal Institution in Transition. 27 min., b&w, 1975. Audio-Visual Center, University of Kansas, 6 Bailey Hall, Lawrence, Kans. 66044.

Administrators, correctional officers, and inmates at the Kansas State Penetentiary, Lansing, present a frank discussion of the prison system. A documentary filmed inside the prison.

Library Inside. 7 min., sound-slide program, 1978. Available from Peter Losi, Institutional Librarian, Buffalo and Erie County Public Library, Lafayette Square, Buffalo, N.Y. 14203. (716) 856–7525.

Depicts library services to the Erie County Correctional Center, which has a library inside.

Life on Death Row. 9 min., b&w, 1968. Indiana University, Bloomington, Ind. 47401.

The experience of living in a cell on Death Row in California's San Quentin Prison is explored in this film.

Like a Rose. 23 min., b&w, 1975. Tomato Productions Inc., Box 1952, Evergreen, Colo. 80439.

A documentary film about the existence of two women serving 25-year sentences in Missouri.

Man to Man. 60 min., color, 1974. WKYC-TV, 1403 E. 6th St., Cleveland, Ohio 44114.

Dramatizes the harshness of prison life, focusing on the hopes of inmates to leave prison and the actual results of the man-to-man reform project.

Maximum Security. 10 min., color, 1978. Distributed by Australian Film Commission, 9229 Sunset Blvd., Los Angeles, Calif. 90069.

Illustrates the heavy psychological and physical stress of maximum-security confinement.

Men in Cages. 52 min., b&w, 1966. Carousel Films, 1501 Broadway, New York, N.Y. 10023.

Investigates living conditions and rehabilitation methods in penal institutions throughout the United States. Interviews first offenders, long term inmates, penologists, directors of state and federal prisons.

National Institute on Library Service to Jail Populations. Videotapes, color. For information on availability, write ASCLA, American Library Association, 50 E. Huron St., Chicago, IL 60611.

Videotapes of presentations at the National Institute, held at Huntsville, Texas, March 9–12, 1980, including: "Overview of the Jail—Trends and Issues"; "Overview of Jail Library Service—Trends and Issues"; "An Inside View—Bars and the Library"; "Assessing Library and Information Needs"; "Looking at Service Programs: Reentry Services, Educational Services, Staff Services, Legal Services"; "Support for Your Program: 'Hustling,' The County Scene, State Library Agencies, State Education Agencies, National Endowment for the Humanities, National Institute of Corrections Jail Center"; "Jail Standards and Accreditation"; "Making Standards Work for You."

No Gun Towers . . . No Fences. 30 min., color, 1969. Audio-Visual Center, Indiana University, Bloomington, Ind. 47401.

Depicts the Robert F. Kennedy Youth Center in Morgantown, West Virginia, as one of minimum security which stresses freedom and responsibility for its "students" who are serving federal sentences. Groups of students with similar behavioral problems live together in cottages.

No Jail Can Change Me. 30 min., b&w, 1972. Extension Media Center, University of California, Berkeley, Calif. 94720.

An interview in a county jail between a 21-year-old black man who has spent most of his life in institutions and a counselor from a Northern California agency that helps inmates and their families.

Nobody Coddled Bobby. 14 min., color, 1979. CBS News, Columbia Broadcasting, System, 383 Madison Ave., New York, N.Y. 10017.

This *60 Minutes'* segment presents the story of the suicide of a teenage delinquent sentenced to a state correctional institution in order to focus on prison life and prison's rehabilitative value.

O P Diary. 30 min., color, 1974. WKYC-TV, 1403 E. 6th St., Cleveland, Ohio 44114.
Follows temporary inmates at Ohio Penitentiary as they experience the injustices and hardships of prison life.

The Odds Against. 32 min., b&w, 1966. American Foundation Institute of Corrections, 1532 Philadelphia National Bank Building, Philadelphia, Pa. 19017.
John Mitchell, 22 years of age, is arrested, tried, convicted, and imprisoned for burglary. Focusing on Mitchell, this documentary explores correctional procedures in the United States today.

On a Question of Justice. 28 min., color, 1975. Films Incorporated, 1144 Wilmette Ave., Wilmette, Ill. 60091.
This film centers on the inequity of sentencing. Sentences for similar crimes vary from judge to judge and are affected by such factors as where the crime was committed, how crowded the court calendar was, even how the judge felt that day. Once in prison the inmates invariably discover this fact.

Penology: The Keepers of the Keys. 22 min., color, 1971. Document Associates, 573 Church St., Toronto, Ontario, Canada.
This film discusses the failures of the present system of penology and examines possible alternatives for the future, including: group therapy sessions; a student program in a minimum security prison; a work release program; and private cottage living in a California prison.

Prison. 58 min., b&w, 1971. Indiana University, Bloomington, Ind. 47401.
Documents life and conditions in a large county jail and rehabilitation center in Pennsylvania. The warden is shown to be concerned with conditions and treatment of the prisoners.

Prison. 10 min., color, 1977. Contemporary/McGraw-Hill Films, Princeton-Hightstown Road, Hightstown, N.J. 08520.
Produced by the National Film Board of Canada, this animated film is about a prisoner's reactions to his first imprisonment. Shows him becoming increasingly more confused and alienated while caught between the behavioral code imposed by the authorities and that imposed by the other convicts.

Prison Community. 29 min., b&w, 1967. International Film Bureau, 332 S. Michigan Ave., Chicago, Ill. 60604.
Demonstrates how a society of prison inmates can become very strong, dominating the attitudes of all prisoners.

A Prison Film: No Walls. 26 min., color, 1971. Churchill Films, 662 N. Robertson Blvd., Los Angeles, Calif. 90069.
A close-up look at a minimum security prison that is a joint venture of the Division of Forestry and the Department of Corrections in California. A film that reflects the attitudes of inmates and officials.

A Prison Film: Still Living. 27 min., color, 1971. Churchill Films, 662 N. Robertson Blvd., Los Angeles, Calif. 90069.
An intimate portrait of a prison environment. Individual inmates and staff members of a women's prison express their attitudes, concerns, doubts, and hopes.

Prisoners. 30 min., color, 1971. Impact Films, 144 Bleecker St., New York, N.Y. 10012.
Features black and white prisoners expressing their views on morals, self-respect, sex, homosexuality, and the prison process, which they feel strips them of their self-esteem.

Rahway, Stay 'Way. 27 min., color, 1977. Films Incorporated, 733 Green Bay Road, Wilmette, Ill. 60091.

Explains a Rahway State Prison (N.J.) program that brings delinquency-prone teenagers inside the prison to learn what confinement is really like. Shows the prisoners graphically describing the horrors of prison life and the stunned reactions of the young people.

Release. 28 min., color, 1974. Odeon Films, 1619 Broadway, New York, N.Y. 10019.

Documentary about a Latino woman who lives in a half-way house with other women just released from jail.

The Reluctant Delinquent. 24 min., color, 1977. Lawren Productions Inc., P.O. Box 666, Mendocino, Calif. 95460.

Portrays the relationship of delinquency to learning disabilities in the case of a young man locked up in a maximum-security facility for juveniles. After years of failure in school, he is learning to read in special education classes.

The Repeater. 20 min., color, 1971. Praxis Productions.

A study of the psychology and culture of prison life as revealed in the actions and reactions of a released prisoner who returns to prison after a period outside.

The Revolving Door. 28 min., b&w, 1968. American Foundation Institute of Corrections, 1532 Philadelphia National Bank Building, Philadelphia, Pa. 19107.

A well-documented film depicting our need for more adequate jail systems. Shows a petty offender, the mechanism of the lower courts and the conditions in local jails. Advocates an effective probation system.

Scared Straight. 54 min., color, 1978. Pyramid Films, P.O. Box 1048, Santa Monica, Calif. 90406.

Presents a documentary about a program in which adolescent offenders visit Rahway prison in New Jersey and observe the realities of life in a maximum-security prison. Shows how a group of criminals serving life sentences convince young delinquents to obey the law.

Short Ice to the Blocks. 6 min., sound-slide program, 1978. Available from Peter Losi, Institutional Librarian, Buffalo and Erie County Public Library, Lafayette Square, Buffalo, N.Y. 14203. (716) 856–7525.

Describes types of materials provided to local adult correctional facilities, including sex-related materials.

Shotgun Joe. 25 min., color, 1970. Jason Films, 2621 Palisade Ave., Riverdale, N.Y. 10463.

Joe Scanlon is serving prison time for armed robbery. The film includes interviews with guards, teachers, inmates, family, and Joe himself that show that he is moving toward self-destruction. A psychological-sociological study.

Squires of San Quentin. 30 min., color, 1978. Motorola Productions, 4825 N. Scott St., Suite 26, Schiller Park, Ill. 60176.

Deals with workshops for adolescent delinquent boys sponsored by the inmates of San Quentin.

Stanford Prison Experiment: A Simulation Study of the Psychology of Imprisonment. Slide/tape, 52 min., 1970. Stanford University, Stanford, Calif. 94305.

A documentation of a psychology experiment administered by Professor Philip Zimbardo at Stanford University, California, in 1970. Eighteen volunteer male college students were randomly divided into guards and inmates and forced to live in a simulated prison environment. The results of this experiment were startling.

The Story of a Prisoner. 26 min., b&w, 1967. Wolper Productions, 8489 W. 3rd St., Los Angeles, Calif. 90048.

The film documents a day in the life of San Quentin prison inmate Jim Britt by showing his work and school routine, a group therapy session, a visit from his wife, his interview with the parole board, and his reaction to the board's verdict.

Tattoo My Soul, Made Straight My Mind. 28 min., color, 1971. Windham School District, Texas Dept. of Corrections, P.O. Box 99, Huntsville, Tex. 77340.

Presents classroom scenes from the Windham School District, a prison-wide program in Texas for over 7,000 students.

This Child Is Rated X. 52 min., color, 1972. National Broadcasting Co., 30 Rockefeller Plaza, New York, N.Y. 10020.

This study of the abuse of children's rights focuses on two types of offenders: the child who has committed a child's crime such as truancy and the child who has committed serious crime. Both often end up receiving the same dehumanizing treatment.

Three Days in the County Jail. 19 min., color, 1975. Disney Educational Media Co., 500 S. Buena Vista Ave., Burbank, Calif. 91503.

The film follows a young man as he is booked in a county jail, encounters the prisoners, and accepts the opportunity to work on an honor farm and to work toward his high school diploma.

Three Thousand Years and Life. 42 min., color, 1973. Odeon, Box 315, Franklin Lakes, N.J. 07417.

During a three-month crisis at the maximum security state prison in Walpole, Massachusetts, the convicts formed a union and took responsibility for administering nearly all functions in the prison.

Time Has No Sympathy. 26 min., color, 1975. Serious Business, 1609 Jaynes St., Berkeley, Calif. 94703.

A straightforward cinema-verite look at the women's section of the San Francisco County Jail. The inmates, mostly young and black, talk about how they got to prison, the tedium and tension of prison life, and their hopes for the future.

Time off the Streets. 34 min., color, 1974. David G. Harris.

Takes a look inside Ontario prisons.

The Tombs. 20 min., 1972. Phil Parmet, 189 S. Harrison St., Princeton, N.J. 08540.

"The Tombs" is the traditional name for the Manhattan House of Detention, where legally innocent men are "detained"—sometimes for years—while awaiting trial.

Two Years or More. 27 min., color, 1970. International Film Bureau, 332 S. Michigan Ave., Chicago, Ill. 60604.

Portrays the life of a prison inmate in old and modern Canadian penitentiaries.

Vermont State Prison. 20 min. Larry Rosenstock, 365 Western Ave., Cambridge, Mass. 01129.

The vicious circle of daily life in America's oldest functioning prison is told entirely in the men's own words. Uniquely, this film is made up of videotaped rap sessions done by the prisoners themselves.

Violent Youth—The Unmet Challenge. 23 min., color. Atlanta Films, 340 E. 34th St., Dept. VY, New York, N.Y. 10016.

This film concentrates on youths from poor economic and social environments and disorganized, turbulent family situations, who are seen as contributors to the rising rates of violent crimes.

Voices Inside. 22 min., color, 1969. Films Incorporated, 1144 Wilmette Ave., Wilmette, Ill. 60091.

Voices of men and women in the United States prison system express their feelings as they show how they live in abject humiliation and degradation. Speaks to the lack of medical care, lack of mental stimulation, and the sexual frustration of prison life.

We're Alive. 50 min., b&w, 1975. Iris Films, P.O. Box 26463, Los Angeles, Calif. 90026.
   Produced by the UCLA Women's Film Workshop and the Video Workshop in the California Institution for Women, this video-film powerfully conveys the thoughts and feelings of the women inside CIW.

Who Is Tracy Williams? 28 min., b&w, 1973. Psych Cinema Register, AV Services, Pennsylvania State University, 17 Willard Building, University Park, Pa. 16802.
   Focuses on the problems, frailties, and strengths of Tracy Williams, an inmate of the State Correctional Institution at Muncy, Pennsylvania. Depicts prison routine.

With Intent to Harm. 28 min., color, 1972. American Friends Service Committee, 48 Inman St., Cambridge, Mass. 02139.
   The first film made entirely inside Massachusetts state prisons. Conditions inside Walpole, Norfolk, Concord, and Framingham are explored.

Women in Prison. 54 min., color, 1974. Carousel Films, 1501 Broadway, New York, N.Y. 10036.
   Revealing survey of conditions in three women's prisons: Los Angeles, Alderson, Virginia, and Marysville, Ohio. Notes that most of the women have been convicted of such crimes as prostitution, drug use, larceny, forgery, and fraud.

Women Inside. 60 min., color, 1979. WNET/13, 356 W. 58th St., New York, N.Y. 10019.
   An interview with inmates at the Dade County (Fla.) Women's Detention Center in Miami. Most of them are serving time for nonviolent crimes involving prostitution, narcotics, or both. The prisoners speak openly of their families, home environments, life in the streets—and why they repeat their offenses.

Yo! Library Man. 8 min., sound-slide program, 1979. Available from Peter Losi, Institutional Librarian, Buffalo and Erie County Public Library, Lafayette Square, Buffalo, N.Y. 14203. (716) 856–7525
   Describes library services provided to the Erie County Holding Center and the Eric County Correctional Center—book cart service and an inhouse library. Inmates' voices and photographs inside the jail provide the tone of being inside.

Further Readings

Bay Area Reference Center. *An Outline of How to Plan a Workshop.* 2nd rev. ed. San Francisco: BARC, San Francisco Public Library, 1979.

Bradford, Leland P. *Making Meetings Work: A Guide for Leaders and Group Members.* San Diego: University Associates, 1976.

Conroy, Barbara. *Library Staff Development and Continuing Education: Principles and Practices.* Littleton, Colo.: Libraries Unlimited, 1978.

Davis, Larry N. *Planning, Conducting, Evaluating Workshops.* Austin, Tex.: Learning Concepts, 1974.

Hart, Lois B., and Schleicher, J. Gordon. *A Conference and Workshop Planner's Manual.* New York: AMACOM, American Management Association, 1979.

Mager, Robert F. *Preparing Instructional Objectives.* 2nd ed. Palo Alto, Calif.: Fearon-Pitman, 1975.

Michigan Library Association Workshop Manual. Lansing: Michigan Library Association, 1977.

O'Neill, Michael E., and Martensen, Kai R. *Criminal Justice Group Training—A Facilitator's Handbook.* San Diego: University Associates, 1975.

Schindler-Rainman, Eva, and Lippitt, Ronald. *Taking Your Meetings Out of the Doldrums.* San Diego: University Associates, 1975.

Warncke, Ruth. *Planning Library Workshops and Institutes.* Chicago: American Library Association, 1976.

Zachert, Martha Jane. *Simulation Teaching of Library Administration.* New York: Bowker, 1975.

Designed by Vladimir Reichl
Composed by FM Typesetting in Linotype Century Schoolbook with
 Helvetica display type
Printed on 50-pound Antique Glatfelter, a pH-neutral stock, and bound
 by the University of Chicago Printing Department